What Peopl[illegible] Apostle Guillermo Maldonado and *Created for Purpose*...

Your life has significance because you were created by God with a purpose. One fundamental task we have as believers is to discover our purpose. But another important assignment is to learn how to *achieve* that purpose. In his book *Created for Purpose,* Apostle Guillermo Maldonado clearly explains the process that is necessary to make it all the way to the finish line of a successful life!

—*Dr. Rod Parsley*
Pastor and founder, World Harvest Church, Columbus, OH

One of the powerful truths presented in *Created for Purpose* by Apostle Guillermo Maldonado is that our divine purpose is always intimately related to the advancement of God's kingdom. This key principle teaches us not to focus on what we *lack* in life—what we don't have and what we think we can't do—but to make all our decisions and plans based on our *purpose.* This approach will open the door to God's provision in all areas of your life and lead you to pursue your God-given purpose with passion. You don't have to hold back on the purpose the Lord has placed in your heart. *Created for Purpose* shows you how He has given you everything you need for all that He has called you to do.

—*Paula White-Cain*
Paula White Ministries
Evangelist and senior pastor
New Destiny Christian Center, Orlando, FL

Believers sometimes run aimlessly through life with no true compass to guide them in their journey. Not knowing our purpose is one of the worst situations we can be in. But finally, there is no longer an excuse! Apostle Guillermo Maldonado has given us a blueprint for discovering and becoming all that God has created us to be. *Created for Purpose* will help equip thousands of believers in Christ Jesus to fulfill their God-ordained destiny!

—Dr. James W. Goll
Author, speaker, communications trainer, and recording artist
God Encounters Ministries

In *Created for Purpose,* Guillermo Maldonado architects a clear plan for how to discover your purpose. You will be so glad you read it! This book will help you avoid getting stuck in life without a defined purpose—or pull you out of the trenches if you haven't gotten very far in understanding your calling. God has an original intention for everything He created, and we have the Bible and His voice to help define His specific intention for us. *Created for Purpose* opens your eyes to see your destiny and then provides practical steps for how to walk it out. It's your time to feel empowered for God's full purpose in your life!

—Shawn Bolz
Host, *Translating God* television program
Host, *Exploring the Prophetic* podcast
Author, *Translating God, God Secrets,* and *Through the Eyes of Love*
www.bolzministries.com

Apostle Guillermo Maldonado has been a spiritual son to me for many years. He is one of the most committed believers I have ever known, and frankly, he is a spiritual genius. His book *Created for Purpose* demonstrates how we are all concerned about understanding our destiny and having a clear vision, and I know the keys in this book will give you great assurance in these vital areas of your life.

—*Marilyn Hickey*
Marilyn Hickey Ministries

CREATED *for*

GUILLERMO MALDONADO

WHITAKER HOUSE

Unless otherwise indicated, all Scripture quotations are taken from the *New King James Version*, © 1979, 1980, 1982, 1984 by Thomas Nelson, Inc. Used by permission. Scripture quotations marked (KJV) are taken from the King James Version of the Holy Bible. Scripture quotations marked (NIV) are taken from the *Holy Bible, New International Version*®, NIV®, © 1973, 1978, 1984, 2011 by Biblica, Inc.® Used by permission of Zondervan. All rights reserved worldwide. www.zondervan.com. The "NIV" and "New International Version" are trademarks registered in the United States Patent and Trademark Office by Biblica, Inc.®

Boldface type in the Scripture quotations indicates the author's emphasis.
The forms *Lord* and *God* (in small caps) in Bible quotations represent the Hebrew name for God *Yahweh* (Jehovah), while *Lord* and *God* normally represent the name *Adonai*, in accordance with the Bible version used.

The definition of the Greek word for *predestined, proorizō*, is taken from the electronic version of *Strong's Exhaustive Concordance of the Bible*, STRONG (© 1980, 1986, and assigned to World Bible Publishers, Inc. Used by permission. All rights reserved.). The definition of the Greek word for *transformed, metamorphoo*, is taken from the resources of biblestudytools.com.

The definitions of *destine* and *predestine* are taken from *Collins English Dictionary* – Complete & Unabridged 2012 Digital Edition, © William Collins Sons & Co. Ltd. 1979, 1986, © HarperCollins Publishers 1998, 2000, 2003, 2005, 2006, 2007, 2009, 2012. Other definitions are taken from Merriam-Webster.com, 2019, http://www.merriam-webster.com.

ERJ editor: Jose M. Anhuaman
Editorial development: Gloria Zura
Cover design: Caroline Pereira

Created for Purpose

Guillermo Maldonado
13651 S.W. 143rd Ct., #101
Miami, FL 33186
http://kingjesusministry.org/
www.ERJPub.org

ISBN: 978-1-64123-337-8
eBook 978-1-64123-338-5
Printed in the United States of America

Whitaker House
1030 Hunt Valley Circle
New Kensington, PA 15068
www.whitakerhouse.com

Library of Congress Control Number: 2019948646

1 2 3 4 5 6 7 8 9 10 11 WH 26 25 24 23 22 21 20 19

CONTENTS

PREFACE

THE GREATEST TRAGEDY IN LIFE IS NOT DEATH
BUT LIVING WITHOUT PURPOSE.

PREFACE

Sooner or later, we all ask ourselves the reason for our existence. Many people never find a satisfactory answer to this question because they are looking in the wrong places. That answer can be found only in the One who created us—God, our heavenly Father.

The truth is, you are a glorious creation of God with a unique and eternal purpose. This means that you are not an accident. Your presence on this earth is not a mistake. Neither is it insignificant. You are wanted here—and needed!

Yet Satan, the enemy of our souls, works incessantly to rob us of our identity, purpose, potential, and destiny because he wants to stop the advancement of God's kingdom on earth. That is why, after we understand our significance as children of God, it is necessary for us to receive a revelation of our calling and destiny, and then begin to walk it out in the power of God's Spirit.

The Holy Spirit inspired my heart to write *Created for Purpose* to share this revelation that God has a purpose for every person's life. This book began with God's work in my own life, in which He revealed my purpose in Him and the process by which we come to understand our purpose. I can't keep this treasure to myself! I have never acted selfishly with what God has given me. I want to share this knowledge so that thousands, perhaps millions, of people in this generation and the ones to come can know their purpose and reach their destiny.

In these pages, you will find topics such as God's original intention for every human being, how to position ourselves in our purpose, and how to follow the path to fulfilling it. I talk about the vital process of forming our character, the anointing that empowers us to accomplish our purpose, how to live for a purpose rather than for a need, and the indicators that allow us to identify our calling. I believe that reading this book will be the beginning of a supernatural journey in your life. Once you know your purpose, you will never go back to the way you used to live!

Dive deeply into this revelation. It will help you make sense of what has happened in your life in the past, and it will give you a future and a hope for the rest of your life—on into eternity. It will lead you to wake up every day full of energy, joy, and happiness. You will no longer live in a state of depression, boredom, or loneliness because being in God's purpose fills us with His eternal life.

WE ARE DIFFERENT ONLY WHEN WE MAKE A DIFFERENCE.

You did not arrive on this earth by chance, and you are not here by accident or as the result of an error. God created you with an intentional and specific purpose so that His kingdom can advance, filling the earth with His joy, love, and peace.

Come to know your purpose and enter into a glorious destiny today, here and now!

GOD'S ORIGINAL INTENT

WHEN OUR LIVES LACK MEANING,
TIME ITSELF CAN BECOME A DIFFICULT BURDEN.

1

GOD'S ORIGINAL INTENT

One of the biggest problems many people face today is not a lack of time, although they may think that's the issue. Rather, it is the exhaustion and emptiness they feel—even after working hard and being involved in many activities and tasks—because they don't have a clear direction in life or know what they really want to achieve.

When we don't know our purpose, it is like trying to push against the heavy waves of the sea or like walking around aimlessly—we never get anywhere. I believe such a lack of purpose is the reason for the increasing number of suicides in the United States in recent years.[1] When people don't know what to live for, death can seem appealing to them. But when they take their own life, they go from human uncertainty into a spiritual realm that is unknown to them.

Sadly, a large percentage of men and women die without understanding why God created them or discovering their purpose on earth. When our lives lack meaning, time itself can become a difficult burden

1. Holly Hedegaard, M.D., Sally C. Curtin, M.A., and Margaret Warner, Ph.D., "Suicide Mortality in the United States, 1999–2017," Centers for Disease Control and Prevention, https://www.cdc.gov/nchs/products/databriefs/db330.htm.

to carry. In contrast, those who know their purpose walk safely through life and are even pursued by success. When I refer to "success," I do not necessarily mean achieving fame or becoming rich, especially since both of these conditions tend to occupy the lowest rungs on the happiness scale. True success comes from doing the will of God and fulfilling the purpose for which we were created. Everything else is extra.

Successful people conquer kingdoms, create nations, and shape history. History does not make them; on the contrary, they make history. Moses freed the Hebrews from slavery, defeating the Egyptian kingdom in the process, and established a new nation—Israel—shaping the course of God's people in history. Jesus Christ, by dying on the cross and rising from the dead, overcame the kingdom of darkness, brought the kingdom of God to earth, and divided the history of humanity into two: before Christ and after Christ.

But it is not only great figures like Moses or Jesus who make their mark on history. When any person dares to think and live differently from the norm, obeying God and following His purposes, they will leave their own mark on the world. If you want to influence the history of your life and that of your family, your city, and even your nation, you have come to the right place. *Created for Purpose* will guide you in how to produce that kind of influence and change!

LONELINESS IS NOT A LACK OF COMPANY; IT IS NOT KNOWING THAT EVERYONE HAS A PURPOSE IN LIFE, COMPLEMENTARY TO THAT OF OTHERS.

GOD CREATED EVERYTHING WITH PURPOSE

Every human being wants to know the purpose for their existence. In fact, there are four main questions that all we seek to answer for our lives: (1) "Who am I?" This is a question of identity. (2) "Where do I come from?" This is a question of origin. (3) "Why am I here?" This is a question of purpose. (4) "Where am I going?" This is a question of destiny. We will experience genuine happiness when we find the answers to these crucial questions. And the only one who can reveal the answers to us is our Creator.

People who lack purpose often do not understand or accept themselves, so they end up competing with those around them. They will try to imitate someone else's appearance, seek to take the place that belongs to another, or attempt to steal the blessings that have been poured out on others. Such competition arises from a missing sense of identity and an ignorance of the fact that each individual has a distinct purpose in life. Those who do not know their purpose will always be insecure.

God has a purpose for everyone and everything He created. We can define purpose as "the original intent or reason for which something was created." In the case of human beings, our purpose is the original intent of God—His determination and desire for us when He gave us life. When I refer to our "creation" by God, I am not talking primarily about our earthly birth, but rather our design by Him in eternity, outside of the *kronos,* or chronological time, that we function under in the world.

Thus, contrary to what many people think, life begins in heaven, not on earth. God designed us in heavenly places before we came to live on the earth. As He told the prophet Jeremiah, *"Before I formed you in the womb I knew you; before you were born I sanctified you; I ordained you a prophet to the nations"* (Jeremiah 1:5). Since everything in God begins with His original intention, we were a fully formed idea in His mind before we ever received our physical bodies. Therefore, we can say that, before we are born, we already "are"—and we have already been given a unique purpose by our Creator.

Seeing things in this way, we must conclude that abortion is a sin, not only because it is the taking of a human life, but also because it is an attack on a divine purpose. No matter how many weeks or months a fetus has gestated, he or she is a person, has life, and was created by God with a purpose. Nobody has the right to truncate that divine purpose.

Purpose gives our lives significance because, once we follow it, we begin to make a difference in the world. Without purpose, our day-to-day life lacks meaning; it becomes merely the passage of time. In effect, those who live without knowing their purpose act irresponsibly because they do not know how to properly value their life, and they end up wasting it. This is the reason why many people are unhappy, dissatisfied, empty, unfocused, depressed, and alone.

Furthermore, God has given each human being a period of time to fulfill their purpose on earth. That is why it is necessary for us to understand and start to follow that purpose as soon as possible. We cannot waste time! We must live with a clear and

PURPOSE LIVES IN THE MIND OF THE CREATOR; THEREFORE, WE ARE A THOUGHT OF GOD IN ACTION.

defined mission for our lives. The Bible states, *"To everything there is a season, a time for every purpose under heaven"* (Ecclesiastes 3:1). It is time to discover your purpose and begin to achieve it!

THE BREATH OF LIFE

In Genesis 1:26, God said, *"**Let Us make man in Our image**, according to Our likeness; let them have dominion over the fish of the sea, over the birds of the air, and over the cattle, over all the earth and over every creeping thing that creeps on the earth."* Then, in Genesis 2:7, we read, *"The LORD God formed man of the dust of the ground, and breathed into his nostrils the breath of life; and man became a living being."* God is a spiritual Being, and these verses affirm that man was first created as a spiritual being in His image, and then was given physical form out of the dust of the earth. It was only when God breathed His *pneuma*, or "breath," of life, into the body made of dust that man was given physical life.

This shows us that, from the beginning of time, humanity has lived in two worlds: the spiritual and the physical. The spiritual world was as real as the natural world. The first human beings, Adam and Eve, maintained communion with God in the garden of Eden, which was the atmosphere of His presence. This communication took place through the spiritual part of their being.

The spiritual world is just as real now as it was then. The great difference between then and now is that, sometime after creation, the spirit of human beings died because of their sin, or rebellion against God. (See Genesis 3.) In a state of spiritual death, it is difficult for a person to access the original heavenly atmosphere for which they were created. That is why it was necessary for God's Son Jesus to come to earth. The spirit of any person can only come alive again in Christ Jesus. (See, for example, Ephesians 2:5; Colossians 2:13.) He rescues us from the world of sin and enables us to live in the atmosphere of heaven, where we can have continual access to the Father and the realm of His Spirit.

GOD ESTABLISHES THE END FROM THE BEGINNING

To live according to our purpose, we must understand that God never does anything as merely a test or an experiment—that when He creates something, it is because He has already given it a purpose and knows exactly how His creation will respond. "[God] *chose us in Him before the foundation of the world, that we should be holy and without blame before Him in love, having* ***predestined*** *us to adoption as sons by Jesus Christ to Himself, according to the good pleasure of His will*" (Ephesians 1:4–5).

To grasp this passage, we first need to explore what it means to be "*predestined*." The original Greek word means "to determine beforehand" or "to ordain." This idea indicates "to give an end or destiny to." One's destiny is guided by a series of invariable outcomes that lead a person to their goal or end. Therefore, "to predestine" someone is to establish their end from the beginning or to decree their destiny in advance.

This is the way God works in our lives: "*For I am God, and there is no other; I am God, and there is none like Me, declaring the end from the beginning, and from*

EVERY PERSON HAS BEEN CREATED WITH A PURPOSE AND IS CALLED ACCORDING TO THAT PURPOSE.

ancient times things that are not yet done, saying, 'My counsel shall stand, and I will do all My pleasure'" (Isaiah 46:9–10).

God predetermined when and how He would save human beings from sin and death—and the enemy, Satan, who opposes God, could not prevent that from happening. Jesus Christ, God's Son—who is fully divine and fully human—died on the cross on a specific day in human history, according to the *kronos* time that governs the earth. However, in eternity, His life had already been delivered for the salvation of the entire human race. He is *"the Lamb slain from the foundation of the world"* (Revelation 13:8). The Word of God declares that only by the work of the cross can we be *"redeemed…from* [our] *aimless conduct…with the precious blood of Christ, as of a lamb without blemish and without spot. He indeed was* ***foreordained before the foundation of the world****, but was manifest in these last times for* [us]" (1 Peter 1:18–20).

When the Scriptures say that we were predestined, they emphasize that God has a purpose for each one of us. We were created in eternity, in a spiritual environment, before the foundation of the world, to have an exclusive destiny previously traced in the mind of God. There are no coincidences in Him. Anything that He formed was first finished in His supernatural mind. He determines the purpose and then shapes the one who will fulfill it. We need to discover and live out the purpose He has for us. However, we must keep in mind that God has also given human beings free will. His ultimate plans for humanity will always come to pass. It is up to us whether we will participate in those plans or forfeit our place in them.

We exist because it is the supreme desire of God for us to be here. Most human beings believe that they exist to satisfy their own selfish desires, but in reality, we exist to satisfy and please God. God is not selfish, and His unconditional love seeks the good of all mankind. His plans for us are better than any personal desires we may have.

YOU ARE NOT AN ACCIDENT

Let's return to a Scripture passage concerning the life of Jeremiah that faithfully expresses the concept of purpose and predestination, as well as the prophetic role that Jeremiah would fulfill in the history of Israel: *"Then the word of the* L*ORD came to me, saying: 'Before I formed you in the womb I knew you; before you were born I sanctified you; I ordained you a prophet to the nations"* (Jeremiah 1:4–5). The phrase *"before I formed you in the womb I knew you"* reveals that this occurred in eternity, outside of measured time. We have seen that the same was true in the life of Jesus, who was sent on a mission to earth from eternity. In Luke 4:43, Jesus talks about a central aspect of that eternal purpose: *"I must preach the kingdom of God to the other cities also, because for this purpose I have been sent."* (See also Mark 1:38.)

No one arrives on earth unless their purpose is already determined in heaven. You are not an experiment or an accident; you are on earth because, in the mind of God, you are already a "finished product," with a purpose and destiny. People may tell you that you are useless and will never be successful in life. The good news is that if you are here, it is because

WE PLEASE GOD BY FULFILLING HIS PURPOSE ON EARTH.

God created you, formed you, and gave you purpose. You are important to His plan!

Never accept other people's negative opinions of you, because nobody knows a finished product better than the One who created it. Additionally, when you walk in God's purpose, you can be assured that everything in your life is working for good: *"And we know that all things work together for good to those who love God, to those who are the called according to His purpose"* (Romans 8:28). God knows why and for what end He created you. If you search for it from your heart, He will reveal to you the purpose of your life, and you can begin to live it out.

In this regard, don't allow the human circumstances of your birth to define you. You might have been born out of wedlock or from a prostitute's womb. You might have been conceived against your mother's will due to rape. Because humanity rebelled against God, we live in a fallen world. God is well aware of the circumstances under which each of us was conceived. Yet in His foreknowledge, He created us all with a purpose—a *good purpose*.

God created you in eternity and gave you a divine destiny. This may explain the course of certain events in your life. Perhaps you almost died in your mother's womb, but you lived, against all odds. Perhaps you were diagnosed with a terminal illness, but you survived. It might be that you were abused, rejected, and mistreated, but you endured. You must realize that God's adversary, the devil, always persecutes those who can ruin his evil plans. However, you are alive now because you have a great purpose, and God fights on your behalf.

Thus, eternally speaking, you are not the product of human invention. You were conceived due to a creative idea from God. No matter what your background, what you must do now is begin to walk through life with the assurance that if God began the work in you, He will finish it. (See Philippians 1:6.) If you don't understand these truths, you will not be able to know or fulfill your purpose.

THE SEED OF POTENTIAL

Almost everything in creation begins in the form of a seed, and each seed represents a potential mature entity that can bear fruit. Furthermore, each fruit that is produced bears its own seeds, so that the original seed is multiplied exponentially. Although this is a natural process in creation, many men and women end their days without bearing fruit and multiplying their "seed."

Like a seed, in order to give life, we must first die to ourselves before we can be reborn and multiply. Jesus said, *"Most assuredly, I say to you, unless a grain of wheat falls into the ground and dies, it remains alone; but if it dies, it produces much grain"* (John 12:24). We see this process in the life of Jesus, who had more followers and produced more miracles through those followers after He died and was resurrected than He had beforehand. His "seed" soon bore a multitude of fruit, and the numerous seeds from that fruit have spread throughout the world—and continue to multiply to this day.

GOD NEVER BEGINS SOMETHING IN TIME UNLESS HE HAS ALREADY FINISHED IT IN ETERNITY.

Some people fail to produce fruit in their lives due to an ignorance of their potential. Others are selfish, not willing to go through the process that enables them to bear fruit—because there is a cost. Still others experience the enemy's attack upon their purpose, and they don't understand how to counteract it. Cemeteries are full of the remains of talented humans who went down to the grave carrying the wisdom they never shared, books or songs they never wrote, inventions they never created, medical breakthroughs they never made, and technology they never developed—good purposes that never saw the light of day.

You were not created just to breathe, eat, and pay bills. Nor were you created just to warm a chair in a church or be merely one of the crowd. You were created for greatness! Just as birds are designed to fly through the sky and fish to swim in the water, you were designed to live in a particular atmosphere—the very presence of God. You were not made for mediocrity; you were made for success. Do not let anything or anyone negate your unique identity. You are a child of God, created with a divine purpose in life. That is a truth that nobody can take from you!

THE DIVINE FORCE OF PURPOSE

While the purpose of every human being is born in heaven, it is essentially carried out on earth. Yet because our purpose originates in God, it is supernatural, and it has a divine force that drives it to fulfillment. How can we know God's purpose for us on earth? How can we know our destiny? By divine revelation, which comes through developing intimacy with God and His Word.

In coming chapters, I will show you how to discern and fulfill the purpose that God has given you. But before we move on, I would like to guide you in two prayers. The first is to receive Jesus into your heart, because our very first purpose as human beings is to love and serve God. (See, for example, Matthew 22:36–38.) Please repeat this prayer out loud:

> Heavenly Father, I recognize that I am a sinner and that my sin separates me from You. I believe that Jesus died for me on the cross and that God the Father raised Him from the dead. Today, I repent of all my sins and voluntarily confess Jesus as my Lord and Savior. I renounce any mind-set that is contrary to Your Word, as well as any agreement with the desires of the sinful nature and with the devil. Instead, I make a covenant with Jesus to love and serve Him. Lord, I ask You to enter my heart and change my life. If I died today, I know I would be in Your arms. Amen!

Now, repeat the following prayer with all of your heart, so that your purpose may be revealed:

> Heavenly Father, I come before Your presence recognizing that I do not know the purpose for which You created me. I acknowledge that it has been difficult for me to submit to the process of dying to myself so that I can fulfill my destiny in You. Today, I surrender in faith, knowing that Your plans for me are better than any self-centered desires I may have. I ask that the Holy Spirit would reveal to me Your purpose for my life, and that You would give me the ability to let

PURPOSE IS THE STARTING POINT WHERE WE SEE THE HAND OF GOD UNFOLDING OUR DESTINY.

go of anything that is not good for me and doesn't build me up. Now, I declare that I will be trained and processed by You, and that I will achieve my purpose in life. Please give me Your grace, Your discernment, and Your power to do great things in my generation. In the name of Jesus, amen!

TESTIMONIES OF FINDING AND FULFILLING PURPOSE

NO GREATER JOY THAN LIVING IN GOD'S WILL

John Laffitte might have become an important NASA engineer, gone to space, and been recognized worldwide; however, he chose to fulfill God's purpose for his life instead. For nearly a decade, he has helped thousands of people transform their lives, teaching the Word of God with revelation and demonstrating the supernaturality of God.

> Growing up, I knew that everyone had a purpose, but I could not prove it. I did not know how to find it, and I did not know of anyone who could teach me. The only guides I had were my parents, and they always told me that I should do something for the good of humanity. At school, I realized that I was a good student, and it was easy for me to achieve good grades. I continually challenged myself with increasingly more difficult courses. I was a logical thinker, yet I was too shy to speak in front of people.
>
> I decided to study aerospace engineering and become an astronaut, graduating from MIT and the University of Michigan. However, as I continued my studies, I had a supernatural encounter with God. The Lord placed in me a deep hunger for His Word, and I studied it continuously for three years. I did not know that He was preparing me for

A PERSON WHO IS NOT WALKING IN THEIR PURPOSE WILL ALWAYS FEEL MISPLACED OR ACT IN AN UNTIMELY WAY.

my purpose. I attended a church, and one day they prophesied that I had a call to teach the Word of God. While I listened to that, I still had my own plans.

After graduating, I returned to Miami and began to attend King Jesus Ministry. When Apostle Maldonado met me, he perceived from the Spirit that I had a call to teach the Word of God. Many doors and opportunities opened for me to teach the Word. At that time, I had an excellent job in engineering and good career opportunities. I made a request to be accepted into the NASA astronaut program, and I was far along in the selection process when God suddenly confirmed His will to me personally, telling me that I should stop those efforts in order to dedicate myself to fulfilling His purpose.

At King Jesus Ministry, I began to volunteer as an interpreter and had the opportunity to be close to a number of men and women of God. Many of them prophesied about my ministerial call. One day, my supervisor at work called me to his office to tell me that they wanted to promote me to vice president with a salary increase. At the same time, Apostle Maldonado asked me to work full-time with him in the ministry. It was time to make a decision: do I follow my own plans or those of God? In that process, I learned that God takes us to a place where we have to choose between doing our will or His.

I turned down the promotion, quit my job, and went to work at King Jesus Ministry. There, I was put in charge of the Supernatural Leadership Institute, and later, the University of the Supernatural Ministry (USM). Over the years, I have seen God move in many powerful ways; and today, we see people around the world moving in His supernatural power, thanks to the training we provide through the institute and university. For example, not long ago, a group of USM students and leaders from our campus in Bolivia went out to evangelize in the streets, demonstrating miracles, signs, and wonders. A young woman prayed for a man who was in a wheelchair in the middle of a plaza. To everyone's amazement, the man got up from the chair, and started running and jumping. This man was very well known in that part of the city. Many people, including the police, gathered in the square because of the news. After seeing this miracle, another twenty people there accepted Jesus as their Lord and Savior.

We have also seen God move in Chiapas, Mexico, thanks to the campus we have in Central America. After taking a course on prayer and being activated to pray for the sick, some of the students visited a hospital and prayed for a man who had been in a coma for fifteen days. The doctors gave no hope for his recovery. However, as the students prayed for this man, the power of God lifted him out of the coma. Shortly thereafter, he was taken out of intensive care and is now recovering. If I had not left my scientific career to dedicate myself to this ministry, I would not be seeing the wonders that God can do through someone who follows His

EVERYTHING ON EARTH MUST GO THROUGH A PROCESS OF NATURAL DEVELOPMENT IN THE DIMENSION OF TIME.

purpose. I have already spent about nine years serving God full-time, but it seems like I started just yesterday.

Now, I understand why God made me the way I am. Being so studious and logical has helped to make me a good teacher of the Word of God. Supernaturally, He removed all fear of speaking in public from me. Now, I can teach or preach in front of thousands of people, and do so with boldness. I can see the hand and blessing of God in my life and in my family. I am also seeing God's supernatural provision, because my daughter received a full scholarship to study at Yale University. There is no greater joy than living in God's purpose for our life. Today, I know that I have entered into my purpose, and I enjoy dedicating my life to helping others enter into theirs.

CALLED TO BE A "SUPERNATURAL DOCTOR"

When Andrew Staiger entered medical school, he was full of doubts about whether he was right for his chosen field. However, he believed in his purpose and persevered. Today, he is one of the best orthopedic surgeons in the world. However, he refers to himself as a "supernatural doctor," a man used by the Lord to rebuild people's hands, while also bringing divine healing to God's people through prayer.

> Becoming a surgeon was an intense struggle for me. I went to several universities until I finished my residency at Southern Illinois University in Springfield, Illinois, which took me five more years. I felt that I should dedicate myself to orthopedic surgery, but I knew it was one of the most competitive specialties that a student can choose. Many times, I questioned God for guiding me to that particular field, and as other students made known their desire to pursue the same specialty, I wanted to switch to something else, but I felt that God did not want me to make a change. So, I continued, and, by the grace of God, I was accepted into a program at the University of Minnesota Medical School. Although this school was not my first choice, it turned out to be the best program for me. It went very well, and as a result, God allowed me to become a surgeon.

THE PROCESS WE GO THROUGH IS DIRECTLY CONNECTED TO OUR FINAL PURPOSE.

During my residency, I faced opposition. I felt persecuted for being a Christian. However, now that I look back on that time, I realize that this was a process in which God was teaching me to interact with my colleagues, to forgive, and not to walk in bitterness. Through this process, God continued to build me to be the surgeon that I am today. He has enabled me to heal people using natural medical means. I have been blessed to be considered one of the best surgeons, if not the best, in my area. However, I feel that this is not just for my benefit, but to help the people who the Lord brings me.

The most common problem a hand surgeon treats is carpal tunnel syndrome, a condition that can be very painful at night. It affects people's use of their hands and functioning in different areas of daily life. Surgically relieving the pressure on the nerve can transform a person's life, because it allows their hand to function normally again. Patients are very grateful. But there are others who come with serious injuries that require surgical correction. They have arthritis in their hands and arms and have suffered a lot of pain, and I know that I can help them. Even though I do so through a natural healing process, the healing still comes from God. Somehow, God is always working through me. I have also been able to see Him using me in a supernatural way.

My wife and I have had the privilege of accompanying Apostle Maldonado to Ethiopia three times for Supernatural Encounter meetings, and I have been able to witness many miracles, signs, and wonders. The first year, we basically served by reviewing testimonies, but I was able to see an amazing miracle in a man who had an injury to his forearm. His tendons and nerves had been cut, and he had lost a large part of the functioning of his hand. Someone prayed for him, and God

WE CANNOT FULFILL OUR PURPOSE UNLESS WE FIRST DIE TO OURSELVES.

restored total functioning to his hand. For me, as a hand surgeon, that was amazing!

On the second trip to Ethiopia, my wife and I were able to pray for people. What struck me most was seeing an old woman sitting on a bench in the middle of the crowd. I asked an interpreter to bring her to me. They brought her in a wheelchair, and I inquired if I could pray for her. She said she had a lot of pain in one leg that made it very difficult for her to stand up. So, I prayed for her through the interpreter. I could discern that an injury to her spine was causing the compression of a nerve. I prayed and asked God to release that nerve, and He did! The woman stood up from the wheelchair and began to walk and then dance, praising God with great joy on her face. I have seen the supernatural power of God move in an incredible way in these encounters. I believe that God did at least seventy miracles of healings and deliverances through us that day.

Because of my hunger for the supernatural, I have always been open to setting aside my natural ability and letting God do the work. Now, He has allowed us to open a House of Peace[2] in our area. We have seen people with

---

2. A House of Peace refers to the home of a member of King Jesus International Ministry who opens his or her doors to receive neighbors, relatives, and friends, with the purpose of sharing the gospel of the kingdom—teaching the Word of God and imparting His power. The same anointing, supernatural power, and presence of God that are found in the main King Jesus Ministry church manifest there.

stage 4 cancer be healed by God after we prayed for them. I believe that when a healing occurs in the natural, it is because, in the supernatural, the afflicted area is already healthy. When we bring God to that process, everything accelerates and becomes more effective, so this has become part of my medical practice.

I still work with natural means, but the supernatural power of God manifests itself on every occasion. I see my patients get healed more quickly and suffer less postoperative pain. God is helping me to change the atmosphere in which I live, so that people can be transformed. So, I can truly say that I am a "supernatural doctor." That is what God has called me to be, that is my purpose, and that is the area in which He has placed me. I am very grateful that God has brought me to Apostle Maldonado, a general of the end times, to be used by Him in this way. It has been a true blessing.

PROCESSED FOR A UNIQUE PURPOSE

THE ASPECTS OF OUR PURPOSE WILL UNFOLD AS WE AWAIT GOD'S EARTHLY TIMING FOR FULFILLMENT.

2

PROCESSED FOR A UNIQUE PURPOSE

In the spiritual dimension, nothing is in the process of being created and nothing will be created in the "future." Everything is fully developed, mature, complete, ready, or formed. Additionally, everything in the spiritual realm is instantaneous, occurring in an eternal present. In contrast, in the natural dimension, we are governed by time. That is why, after being created in heaven, everything that is formed on earth in fulfillment of God's plan requires a process. This includes our life and our purpose.

We need to undergo a process—usually a series of processes—for our purpose to reach maturity or fullness. The aspects of our purpose will unfold as we await God's earthly timing for fulfillment. We carry something powerful from God in the Spirit, but we must be ready to go through His process, so that what has already been created in the spiritual realm can be manifested in the natural realm. We have to be trained to accomplish the purpose for which we were created.

UNDERSTANDING THE PROCESS

What, exactly, does a process involve? *Merriam-Webster* gives these definitions for *process*: "progress"; "advance"; "a natural phenomenon marked by gradual changes that lead toward a particular result"; "a continuing natural or biological activity or function"; "a series of actions or operations conducing to an end." In other words, a process is a continuous series of actions, steps, and changes that lead to a result or destination.

We undergo this process in order to be formed. *Formation* is defined as "an act of giving form or shape to something or of taking form: development." Formation involves a process that is followed until something or someone is fully developed, completed, finished, or trained. In the natural, as children grow, they often feel pain when their bones undergo a growth spurt, because it involves a radical change in their bodies. Growing in our purpose necessitates that we adapt to new levels of maturity, intellect, and character. And without a doubt, we must often go through painful stages involving periods of adjustment and adaptation, until we reach the development and transformation that our purpose requires.

I have found this to be the case in my own life. To become who I am now, to have what I have, and to be in full compliance with my purpose on earth, it has been necessary for me to go through various divine processes. Some have taken days, others have taken weeks or months, and several have taken years. Many of these processes have been painful. Nothing I have achieved has been easy, but the Lord has given me the grace to accomplish it. I have gone through tests, tribulations, persecutions, accusations, opposition, pain, offenses, temptations, wounds, betrayals, and

IN HIS WISDOM, GOD LEADS US TO UNDERGO A PROCESS SO WE CAN REACH MATURITY AND FULFILL HIS PURPOSE FOR US.

sacrifice, but in everything, I have seen the faithfulness of my Lord Jesus Christ. The fruit of these processes has been the development of my purpose. Submitting to God's processes has made me a man who has died to himself and is entirely dedicated to fulfilling His will on earth. I have yielded my life to the Father, declaring, as Jesus did, *"Not My will, but Yours, be done"* (Luke 22:42). Today, I can say that I walk fully in my purpose. *"Giving no offence in any thing, that the ministry be not blamed: but in all things approving ourselves as the ministers of God, in much patience, in afflictions, in necessities, in distresses"* (2 Corinthians 6:3–4 KJV).

THE LAW OF PROCESS

Just as there are universal laws in the natural world, such as the law of gravity or the laws of motion, there are laws in the spiritual world. Universal laws cannot be avoided, annulled, or changed. The law of process is one of them. It is not optional, but rather a law to which every purpose of heaven is subject. It is the means by which something or someone is formed or made, so that it can reach its destiny.

As stated earlier, the law of process rules only in the natural realm because in heaven, everything is completed. Your purpose has already been established. However, now that you have arrived on earth, you must still undergo a process so that you can be prepared for its fulfillment. There is an enormous distance between creation and formation.

In the natural realm, we pass through various processes leading to the full development of our potential as human beings. In terms of our physical development, we begin as an infant, grow to be a child, go through puberty, and become a young adult, until we reach the maturity of full adulthood. A similar process occurs in our spiritual development. We follow a growth process until we reach the necessary maturity that will allow us to complete our purpose.

GOD ALWAYS TRAINS US BEFORE ENTRUSTING US WITH A MINISTRY.

If we don't go through this process, we won't be able to enter into our destiny. Many people know in theory that they were created for a big purpose, but they haven't been taught how to achieve it or what to do with it. Others understand the idea of process, but they aren't willing to submit to it, and so they miss out on their potential.

As you might assume, I did not start out as an apostle. When I received Jesus in my heart and accepted Him as the Lord and Savior of my life, I wanted to do whatever it took to serve Him. So, I began cleaning the bathrooms at the church I attended at the time. I ministered to the young people, I evangelized, I was a translator (English to Spanish), and I was a driver. I helped out wherever I could. After many years, I began to travel as an evangelist to various cities and countries, but I didn't start by speaking at large stadiums. I started by going to small churches in small towns in remote places in Latin America.

Years later, my wife and I felt the call to begin a ministry in the city of Miami. We did not start out in the large, beautiful church with the capacity for thousands of people from which we minister today. No! We began in our home with a congregation of twelve people, to whom we preached the gospel of the kingdom. As the number of attendees grew, we moved to a small building where we worked hard, forming leaders and being trained ourselves. We went through the whole course of growth that God demanded of us. Only in this way could we receive from Him the ministries we oversee today. We submitted to the process of doing things God's way, in order to be formed to fulfill our purpose in His kingdom. During that time, I learned that a person can have full potential according to the world—a great purpose and call, personal charisma, and even many spiritual gifts—but if they do not go through a process that molds their character, gifts, patience, and strength, they will not be able to achieve their purpose.

At this point, you are probably asking yourself, "What will happen to me during this divine process?" "Why does it have to be painful?" "What will be the result of the process?" In this chapter, we will focus on two main facets of the process: the transformation of our spirit, soul, and body; and the development of our character.

THE PROCESS LEADS TO TRANSFORMATION

TRANSFORMATION OCCURS IN OUR TOTAL BEING

Our human spirit, dead because of sin, comes alive when we receive Christ as our Savior, and God's Holy Spirit comes to live inside of us. Then, in the process of transformation, God begins to heal our physical body and our soul—our mind, will, and emotions. He wants us to have a healthy body that is free of all sickness and other unhealthy elements, including demonic spirits of illness and death. Our part in this physical transformation is to make positive, practical choices, such as eating healthy foods, exercising responsibly, and making sure we get enough rest.

God also wants us to have a healthy mind. This includes transforming our thought life and being protected from developing mental conditions such as losing our reasoning capacity or our memory. We cooperate in this process of the transformation of our mind by reading, studying, meditating on, and memorizing God's Word:

> *I beseech you therefore, brethren, by the mercies of God, that you present your bodies a living sacrifice, holy, acceptable to God, which is your reasonable service. And do not be conformed to this world, but be transformed by the renewing of your mind, that you may prove what is that good and acceptable and perfect will of God.*
> (Romans 12:1–2)

Additionally, God desires that we live in a healthy emotional state. As we go through His divine processes, He enables our emotions to be transformed, especially as we learn to receive God's love for us and to forgive others. Even depression and personality disorders can be healed. This happens because the Holy Spirit begins to heal us from the inside out.

TRANSFORMATION IS CONTINUAL AND PROGRESSIVE

The Greek word translated "*transformed*" in the above passage is *metamorphoo,* meaning "to change into another form." This is the same term used to describe Jesus at His transfiguration, where the word is translated as "*transfigured.*" (See Matthew 17:1–2.) Our transformation into the image of Christ is a continuous and progressive process that takes us "*from glory to glory*": "*But we all, with unveiled face, beholding as in a mirror the glory of the Lord, are being transformed into the same image from glory to glory, just as by the Spirit of the Lord*" (2 Corinthians 3:18). The main purpose of process is to achieve a total transformation in our lives. For this reason, breaking the law of process can be lethal to our calling.

THE CONDITION OF YOUR HEART WILL BE THE CONDITION OF YOUR LIFE.

TRANSFORMATION HAS DISTINCT PURPOSES

What can we expect from this process of transformation? Here are some of its divine purposes.

1. *Transformation changes our heart.* The heart is the inner man or the resting place of the presence of God. As we go through the process of change, we must remember that all transformation into the image and likeness of Christ originates in the heart, not in the mind, even though the mind is also renewed. We cannot truly be changed merely by applying a mental understanding of sound principles. We must first be transformed in our spirit. The beginning of transformation therefore occurs when we are born again. Jesus taught this truth to a Pharisee named Nicodemus: "*Most assuredly, I say to you, unless one is born again, he cannot see the kingdom of God*" (John 3:3). Everything that God does in our lives begins in the heart.

When our spirit is renewed in Christ, we can undergo the changes in our minds and emotions we discussed above. For instance, once, I was ministering in our church when the Spirit of God led me to call people who were sick to be prayed for. However, before I began to pray, the Spirit showed me that many of them had a lack of forgiveness in their hearts. When we led them to forgive, more than two hundred people were healed.

2. *Transformation leads us to know God as our total reality.* Our transformation by the Holy Spirit gives us an awareness of the reality of God and enables us to receive revelation of the Father's mind. The enemy wants us to ignore the reality of the spiritual world because then we will not understand his deceitful plans to destroy us and others. The Bible warns, "*My people are destroyed for lack of knowledge*" (Hosea 4:6). But if we allow ourselves to be guided and changed by the Holy Spirit, we will be able to see God in all His splendor in every area of our life and defeat the schemes of the enemy.

WITH TRANSFORMATION, WE BECOME ON EARTH WHAT WE ALREADY ARE IN HEAVEN.

3. *Transformation leads to a demonstration of God's power, dominion, and authority.* The divine process allows us to experience God in the now and manifest His life and power in our environment. The more advanced the transformation of our body, mind, will, and emotions, the more we can demonstrate the power of God and take dominion over creation, spreading God's kingdom with the authority that Jesus won on the cross.

4. *Transformation enables us to become a bearer of the glory of God.* Transformation also brings the presence of God and makes us bearers of His glory. Wherever God's presence is, heaven invades earth, time stops, and God does what man finds impossible. You can become a bearer of the glory of God if you allow yourself to be transformed by the Holy Spirit.

5. *Transformation puts to death the old nature.* Each time we allow the Holy Spirit to bring change and healing to our minds and emotions, more of the power of the old sinful nature within us dies. At the same time, the holy nature of Jesus grows in us until we are transformed into His likeness:

> *Therefore, brethren, we are debtors—not to the flesh, to live according to the flesh. For if you live according to the flesh you will die; but if by the Spirit you put to death the deeds of the body, you will live. For as many as are led by the Spirit of God, these are sons of God.*
>
> (Romans 8:12–14)

THE PROCESS FORMS CHRIST'S CHARACTER IN US

As we become more like Christ, our transformation brings about the development of our personal character. The world is full of good people, but going through divine processes makes the difference between a good man and a man of God, between a good woman and a woman of God. What distinguishes a true man or woman of God is the quality of their character. And having mature character is a foundational condition for fulfilling our eternal purpose on earth.

WHAT IS CHARACTER?

Character, in itself, is the set of qualities a person has that distinguishes them and directs their words and actions. It is what we truly are on the inside, and it is what comes to the surface when we are under pressure. If there is bitterness inside, then bitterness will come out; if there is jealousy inside, then jealousy will come out. This is why it is important for us to submit to the God-given pressures that are part of His process. Only then will we see at what stage in our formation we have arrived. We will know in what ways we have matured and what other qualities we still need to allow God to form in us.

The Bible calls these God-given pressures "trials" or "tribulations." In his letter to the Romans, Paul discussed a primary way in which true Christian character is developed when he wrote, "*...we also glory in tribulations, knowing that tribulation produces perseverance; and perseverance, character; and character, hope. Now hope does not disappoint, because the love of God has been poured out in our hearts by the Holy Spirit who was given to us*" (Romans 5:3–5).

FOLLOWING CHRIST'S EXAMPLE

Paul also wrote this to the believers living in the Roman province of Galatia in Asia Minor: "*My little children, for whom I labor in birth again* *until Christ is **formed** in you...*" (Galatians 4:19). What was the apostle saying? That the character we need in order to fulfill our purpose should resemble that of Christ. That we must be processed until we think, act, respond, and live in the same way that Christ would. We cannot achieve this result in our own human strength or wisdom, because it requires a supernatural transformation that only the Spirit of God can give us.

Jesus Himself did not begin to fulfill His purpose and develop His ministry until His character was formed after undergoing the process of growing from childhood to adulthood:

> *And the Child grew and became strong in spirit, filled with wisdom; and the grace of God was upon Him.... And Jesus increased in wisdom and stature, and in favor with God and men.*
> (Luke 2:40, 52)

Although Jesus is the Son of God, and fully God Himself, while He lived on earth as a man, He did not refrain from going through various processes leading to maturity. During this time, He was being formed by the heavenly Father to fulfill the specific purpose for which He had been sent to the world. If the Son of God's character needed to be formed, what makes us think that we can avoid that process and still achieve our purpose?

In Hebrew culture, a man reached full maturity at about thirty years of age. It is no coincidence that

TRUE TRANSFORMATION IS SUPERNATURAL BECAUSE IT LEADS THE BELIEVER TO ACQUIRE THE IMAGE AND LIKENESS OF CHRIST.

Jesus began His ministry at that same age. After thirty years of formation, He was prepared for these crucial life events: being baptized in the Jordan as an act of fully surrendering to the Father's will; resisting the temptations of Satan in the desert; experiencing transfiguration in God's glory on the mountain; riding victoriously through the streets of Jerusalem on what we now call Palm Sunday; enduring the strain of His last night in the garden of Gethsemane, where He again fully submitted to the will of the Father; going out to meet His betrayer and be arrested; bearing the weight of the cross on the road to Calvary; and giving His life for humanity on that cross. He did all this in full compliance with the will of the Father.

Thus, the main purpose of God's process in our lives is to progressively form us into the image and likeness of Christ. *"For whom* [God] *foreknew, He also predestined* ***to be conformed to*** *the image of His Son, that He might be the firstborn among many brethren"* (Romans 8:29). *"To be conformed to"* is another way of saying that the character of Christ must be formed in each one of us, just as it was in Jesus. To really understand and fulfill our purpose, we must go through the same process of maturity that He went through, and that takes time. The process is ongoing. Without time and continuity, we won't be able to mature in character.

Many people with great gifts and talents have poor character because they have not allowed their character to be formed by God. Character is not measured by the quantity or greatness of our gifts, but by how we react to and grow during times of great pressure or moments of adversity. We are born with our gifts. They are given to us by God's grace, and we do not have to do anything to receive them. But we are not born with mature character, and we have to work on it constantly. Refusing to accept the necessary divine pressure during the process is equivalent to telling God that we do not want to develop our character or reach maturity, and that we do not intend to fulfill His purpose.

Today, many people refuse to go through God's process because the spirit of this century is immediacy. Not many are willing to wait and submit to times of personal growth. Consequently, there is a great deficit in character among our leaders, both in the church and in the rest of society. People want to obtain leadership positions by taking shortcuts that are either unethical or do not prepare them to hold up under pressure and temptation. Few are willing to go through the training process to become effective leaders. As a result, we have corrupt politicians, teachers without morals, arbitrary judges, ministers who have no fear of God, and the list goes on.

If you have not been processed, you are rejecting your purpose. If the process you are undergoing bothers you because you see that someone else's process is different, and you think yours should be easier, you are disregarding and delaying your destiny. One person's process will not be the same as another's because everyone is designed to have their character formed individually, and everyone's purpose is unique. Stop looking at other people's processes and focus on yours!

Let me emphasize once more that to rebel against the process is to go against God Himself and against your purpose. Rebels are those who seek other options to achieve their purpose without going through the mandatory process, who take detours to try to achieve the benefits without having to pay the price. This is a very dangerous practice. Those who achieve success using only their gifts and charisma will be

AFTER A PROCESS OF MATURITY THAT SPANNED THIRTY YEARS, JESUS WAS READY TO FULFILL HIS PURPOSE OF BRINGING THE KINGDOM OF GOD TO EARTH AND DYING ON THE CROSS TO REDEEM HUMANITY.

unable to maintain that success. Their lack of maturity may cause them to lose—sometimes, in an instant—what took them years to build. I know many ministers who have had to pass hard tests, face great failures, and suffer deep humiliations because they did not form their character before launching into pursuing their purpose.

If you tell me that you have been formed as a man or woman of God and are mature, I want to know what your process was, because one cannot exist without the other. The Bible states that *"many are called, but few chosen"* (Matthew 20:16). The reality is that many are called to fulfill a divine purpose, but not everyone agrees to submit to the process of maturity that the call demands. We have to be willing to go through a process that is painful and takes time, patience, and death to self.

Many people fear that they will not be able to hold up under the God-ordained pressure, and they are tempted to leave the process so as not to expose themselves to failure. At such times, we must remember that our heavenly Father is working in our lives and is forming our character for greatness. We must resist the temptation to flee and instead allow ourselves to be molded by Him. During the process, I encourage you to seek the support of other strong believers, maintain your prayer life, and keep reading the Word in order to stay close to God and His will.

Remember, too, that you are not the only one who has gone through this process. In the Bible, we observe that, one after the other, all those chosen by God for His purposes had to go through long processes before they arrived at their destinations. For example, Moses went through a forty-year process before he became the liberator of the Hebrew people. Joseph was processed for thirteen years in Egypt before he became the prime minister of that nation. David went through an up-and-down process for thirty years, from boyhood to adulthood, before he became king of Israel. Jesus underwent thirty years of character preparation before beginning His ministry.

At King Jesus Ministry, we follow this very clear biblical revelation of the law of process. In fact, the vision that God has given us for the discipleship and training of new believers corresponds to the process that each Christian needs to go through in order to achieve their purpose. New believers in our church begin by being baptized in water and receiving the baptism in the Holy Spirit. They continue the process by being taught in the School for New Believers, where they receive the milk of the Word of God so they can learn to walk in their new faith. They go on to join a House of Peace, where they are ministered to, delivered of any demonic oppressions, and given biblical and practical instruction for life. At the same time, they are assigned to a "discipleship"—a one-on-on relationship with a mature believer—where they begin to develop their potential based on their gifts and callings. Then, they are trained to be a House of Peace leader, and finally to become a mentor with their own discipleships, in which they guide new believers to begin a process similar to the one they have gone through. In addition, King Jesus Ministry has established the Supernatural Leadership Institute and the University of the Supernatural Ministry, where believers are trained according to their ministerial calls. During their formation, each believer goes through various personal processes, until they reach the destiny that God has designed for their lives.

GIFTS ARE ACQUIRED BY GRACE, WHILE CHARACTER IS FORMED UNDER PRESSURE.

SAY YES TO GOD'S PROCESS

There is a strong spiritual battle for our hearts taking place: the Spirit of God intercedes for us to keep us in Christ (see Romans 8:26–27), while the enemy seeks to turn us away from God's truth so that we cannot be transformed (see, for example, Matthew 13:19). If we say yes to the deceit and lies of the enemy, we will conform to the world and stop being relevant to God's kingdom. On the other hand, if we say yes to the truth of God, we will be transformed *"from glory to glory"* to achieve a glorious destiny on earth. To say yes to God is to accept the process by which we die to our old nature so that Christ may be formed in us. That is the challenge God puts before you today.

If you understand the virtue of the law of process, recognizing that it will lead you to accomplish your divine purpose, I invite you to say the following prayer out loud. Allow the Holy Spirit to give you the strength and wisdom to submit to your personal processes of transformation.

> Heavenly Father, I come before Your presence acknowledging that I have not known how to submit to the processes that You have put before me to take me to the revelation and accomplishment of my purpose on the earth. Today, I repent of my rebellion, selfishness, pride, and unrenewed mind. I accept Your processes with the goal of being transformed in spirit, soul, and body, of conforming my character to that of Christ's. I want to be a bearer of Your glory and a demonstrator of Your power, dominion, and authority. I want You to be my total reality, and I desire that my heart be changed to align with Yours. Please give me Your grace to surrender my will completely to You and to believe that You will be with me in the processes through which You lead me.
>
> Christ in me is the hope of glory! I know that Your processes will enable me to achieve my purpose and thus reach the

glorious destiny You have for me. I want to be on earth what I am in heaven. Transform my life with your love. In the name of Jesus, amen! (See Colossians 1:27.)

WITH THE LAW OF PROCESS, THERE ARE NO SHORTCUTS.

TESTIMONY OF FINDING AND FULFILLING PURPOSE

A PURPOSE THAT LED TO THE WHITE HOUSE

Paula Michelle White-Cain is a minister of God and is currently a spiritual adviser to the president of the United States of America, Donald J. Trump. The process that the founder of Paula White Ministries had to live through was long and difficult, but she came through it victoriously. And God has opened many doors for her so she could fulfill His purpose for her life.

> In my walk with Christ, I have had many experiences that have led me to depend on Him alone. For years, no one knew about the pain and wounds of my past, or the abuse I suffered in my childhood, for I had kept all of that hidden. Thank God, at age eighteen, I met a gentleman who asked me something very strange: "Do you know who you are, Paula? You are more than a mind and a body. You are a daughter of God, a spiritual being. God has a plan for your life." He was the one who introduced me to Christ and taught me that there was sin in me that separated me from God. I felt that a great force was speaking to me; it was the call of inexplicable love and purity. I cried when I realized how lost I was and how I had lived carrying a big backpack full of pain on my shoulders. I wanted to be free. I had never heard about being born again; neither did I understand what it meant to have a spiritual awakening. The only thing I did at that moment was to believe. I had lived blind for eighteen years, and now I could see.
>
> All my life, I had wanted to be loved, to be cared for, to be protected, and to belong to someone, but none of that had happened for me. However, now, God gave me everything. I started spending time reading the Bible and praying every day. I began

to discover God's promises to me, to develop my faith, and to believe that God can do all that His Word says. I learned that He never leaves you in the condition that causes you pain; He heals every wound. He restores, revives, refreshes, and renews. One night, while I was praying and worshipping, I felt that something was being torn from my whole being. God freed me from many things. A dark and heavy veil was lifted from me, and what had blinded me was shattered by the healing light of God.

At one point, I read a verse that became a guide for my life and sealed my existence: "To Him who is able to do all things much more abundantly than we ask or understand, according to the power that acts in us." (See Ephesians 3:20.) I always felt that God was going to do much more than I could desire of Him, and that what I perceived as greatness was small compared to the immensity that He had destined for me.

One night, I had a divine visitation that changed my life. I fell asleep, and suddenly, in a vision, I was placed on almost every continent of the world, in countries that were very far away. Every time I spoke before a sea of people, something supernatural happened. Millions of men, women, and children listened, looked to God, and found the same life that I had received. They were saved by the Word of God that came from my mouth. All those people found deliverance, restoration, salvation, hope, and healing by the Spirit of God. But when I stopped talking, the crowd quieted and the bright light of hope dimmed. The longer the silence lasted, the more people around me became shadows and sank into darkness. I had to speak, loud and strong, with boldness and great purpose. My heart was pounding; I was in the presence of God, in a holy moment. God wanted me to preach! The next day, I went to see my pastor and told him my vision, explaining that God had called me to preach. He replied, "Wonderful! Our maintenance manager has just left; you can clean the church."

I spent six months on that task, and then I worked in the children's nursery. After that, I was assigned to teach four-year-olds. Following this, I led the young people's group. As the group grew, I was called to be part of the church staff as Director of Evangelism. Then, I got married and prepared to move to Tampa, Florida, where my husband felt he had to serve God. We prayed, we fasted, we sold everything, and we left.

In Tampa, we led Bible studies and ministered to a group of children. We created a program for children in a very dangerous neighborhood where the police only entered with an escort. Sometime later, we started our own church with five people. After more time had passed, we began the season of going out into the world via television; that's how Paula White Ministries was born. God opened doors without precedent, and ministerial opportunities exploded. We had one of the fastest-growing churches in the nation, with more than fifteen thousand people. But while things looked great on the outside, our life began to fall apart on the inside. We faced an endless series of crises that shook our foundation, and I went through a painful divorce.

I left the church, but I continued to minister through Paula White Ministries. One of the cities most impacted by my ministry was New York, where I ended up forming a Bible study for the New York Yankees. I also pastored New Destiny Christian Center in Florida. As Paula White Ministries grew stronger and became a voice to the world, I received a call from Donald Trump. He had seen me on television and had felt the anointing of God on my life, and he invited me to meet his family and his staff.

The second time we met together, the Lord told me, "Show him who I am." I knew it was an assignment from God. So, for many years, I have been a spiritual counselor for Mr. Trump, leading Bible studies, praying, and being a spiritual voice that he hears. Several years before he ran for president of the United States, he began to ask me to pray for that. When he decided to launch his candidacy in 2014, he called and asked me to organize a meeting with pastors and to organize the evangelicals. Then, I understood that it was God's will. I worked arduously with his campaign team. I spent myself working on this assignment, which I now know that God had given me many years earlier. Praying for Mr. Trump is something that I have done since the beginning of our relationship. This is what God planned: that I would enter into

WE HAVE ONLY ONE PURPOSE IN GOD, BUT EACH TIME WE START A NEW SEASON IN OUR LIVES, WE BEGIN A NEW PROCESS.

that relationship without having any idea that he would become the president of my nation.

Almost daily, I remember when I received Jesus as my Lord and Savior. Although, just as it was in the beginning, I do not understand everything, I somehow know that no matter what happens, as long as I remain faithful to His Word and obedient to His call, He will not only sustain me, but will also bless and equip me to fulfill every assignment He gives me. He has never forgotten me. He is the maintainer of my soul and the one who raises my head.

ENTERING INTO THE PROCESS

A HUNGER FOR "MORE" OF GOD IS A SIGN THAT HE IS TAKING US TO A NEW DIMENSION.

3

ENTERING INTO THE PROCESS

We know that there is much more of God that we have not yet experienced. However, we need revelation of what it means to receive more of Him. It does not refer to a petty spirit of accumulation, greed, or hoarding. Rather, this "spirit of more" comes from the Holy Spirit, who is an inexhaustible source and always has more from God for us, not only in material wealth, but also in peace, joy, family unity, health, dreams, ideas, projects, and many other blessings. When we do not have the "spirit of more," frustrations come into our lives, and the "spirit of scarcity" ends up suffocating us—until the day when we get fed up with it, and we determine to be transformed into the image and likeness of Christ.

I am always pushing to break new barriers of growth, anointing, prayer, glory, power, transformation, revelation, knowledge, and learning. I am always open to receiving fresh truths that the Holy Spirit wants to reveal to me. Every day, I am hungry, eager, and passionate for more of God, the kind of hunger that gives wings to the Spirit to take us to new levels in our purpose on earth.

FOLLOWING THE DESTINY OF YOUR LIFE BEGINS WITH THE KNOWLEDGE OF YOUR PURPOSE.

A NECESSARY PATH

As we established in the previous chapter, the law of process is not an option; it is a necessary path for all who want to achieve their purpose and fulfill God's will for their life. God knew our destiny before He created us. Psalm 139:16 says, "*Your eyes saw my unformed body; all the days ordained for me were written in your book before one of them came to be*" (NIV). For this reason, we must yield the conduct of our life to Him. God doesn't usually tell us all that we will need to go through in order to reach our destiny; if He did, we might give up before we started! The truth is that the process always includes a valley of the shadow of death, where we feel that we will never make it out—that everything is finished and we will perish. But it is not the end. It is just a portion of that necessary path, and God is with us every step of the way. That is why the psalmist confidently says, "*Though I walk through the valley of the shadow of death, I will fear no evil; for You are with me; Your rod and Your staff, they comfort me*" (Psalm 23:4). Anyone who has not passed through a valley of the shadow of death has not been processed; therefore, God cannot entrust His purpose to them or take them to their destiny.

THE PROCESS PURIFIES US

To receive more of God and enter into our purpose, we must allow Him to purify us as we are being processed. Without this purification, we will have a mixture of ungodliness and godliness in our character. An Old Testament picture of this mixture is the *"profane* [*"strange"* KJV] *fire"* that the sons of Aaron offered to God in violation of His instructions (see, for example, Leviticus 10:1). Such a mixture contains spiritual impurities, where there is a little bit of God, a little bit of the flesh, and a little bit of the devil. (See Ephesians 2:1–3.) God rejects strange fire because it taints and destroys our purpose while dishonoring Him.

Throughout my ministerial life, I have seen people lose everything because they refused to undergo the process of purification and formation that would take them to their destinies. We cannot play with God! We cannot walk toward our purpose full of impurities—pride, selfishness, and other forms of sin and evil. When we are disobedient to God's Word, we are in danger of experiencing the resulting curses and even destruction. (See Deuteronomy 27–28.) But when we submit to the process, we allow God to cleanse our hearts and purify our motives, so that He may be glorified and our generation may be blessed. So, yield to God, repent of any rebellion and disobedience in your life, and receive His forgiveness and blessings. (See Ephesians 4:22–23.)

THE PROCESS LEADS US TO DIE TO SELF

As part of our purification, we undergo loving discipline from our heavenly Father to remove our self-centeredness and selfish desires. Our fallen human nature demands self-indulgence and has an appetite for all that produces temporary and carnal pleasures. But our purpose cannot be fulfilled under those conditions. God has created us to be a blessing to others and to impact the world with His love and power.

If we do not go through God's process, we cannot change. And if we do not change, we cannot fulfill His plan for us. Remember that Jesus underwent demanding processes before and during His ministry, culminating in His sufferings on the cross. Thanks to these processes,

He became our Savior. He was then exalted by the Father, who made Him King of kings, Lord of lords, and High Priest of mankind. But to reach such a high level, He first *"humbled Himself and became obedient to the point of death, even the death of the cross"* (Philippians 2:8).

To die to ourselves means to stop looking out only for our own interests, to give ourselves to God for the sake of others. But, even more, it means giving up our own will to fulfill God's will. As we learned in chapter 1, to bring about this change in our life, we need to be like a seed that is planted in the earth and dies. That is the highest sacrifice a person can make, but it is done by those who recognize that only the seed that dies can give life. That is why Gethsemane sealed the process in the life of Jesus. (See Matthew 26:36–46.)

THE PROCESS SUSTAINS OUR SUCCESS

Success is our destiny, but we will not be able to sustain it unless we have been processed. I mentioned earlier that our gifts may catapult us to the peak of success, but only character can keep us in that privileged place. What good would it be to achieve success for a short while, only to have everything collapse because we have nothing with which to sustain it? In God, success is genuine and sustainable; therefore, before giving us success, He has to prepare us, change us, and mature us.

THE PERSON WHO IS NOT PROCESSED DOES NOT CHANGE; AND WITHOUT CHANGE, WE CANNOT ACHIEVE OUR LIFE PURPOSE.

THE PROCESS PREPARES US FOR THE ANOINTING

The life of Jesus is always our best example, and this is certainly true with regard to God's anointing on our lives. Jesus went to the Jordan River to be baptized and anointed by God's Holy Spirit so that He would be able to fulfill His purpose on earth. He was not baptized right after He was born; rather, He was baptized thirty years later. One of the reasons why He was processed for three decades is that, if He hadn't traveled that path, He couldn't have carried the anointing God intended for Him.

There are various leaders in the church who have high positions but have never been processed. This situation has the potential to bring terrible consequences to the body of Christ. People are placing their trust in these leaders, and their faith may become damaged or broken if the leaders cannot sustain their success in integrity and grace. It is imperative that these leaders go through a process of sanctification, where they are set apart for the exclusive use of God, so they can carry the anointing and power of Christ as they live a life of honor and trustworthiness.

THE PROCESS CONFIRMS WE ARE PART OF GOD'S REMNANT

I am convinced that from our generation will come the remnant that will prepare the earth for the second coming of the Lord: *"And it shall come to pass that whoever calls on the name of the Lord shall be saved. For in Mount Zion and in Jerusalem there shall be deliverance, as the Lord has said, among the remnant whom the Lord calls"* (Joel 2:32). *"Even so then, at this present time there is a remnant according to the election of grace"* (Romans 11:5). The true remnant will go through a process, because that is what will qualify us to endure and overcome the strong opposition that will arise against the coming of Christ.

HOW TO BEGIN THE PROCESS

Maybe you feel that you know your purpose, but you do not know how to start walking in it through God's process. Let me give you two guidelines to help you do this.

DISCERN YOUR PROCESS

When we yield to God, we are initiated in our purpose. Some people haven't submitted to their processes because they haven't yet recognized them. Process comes to us in various ways, according to the areas in our character that need to be formed. We must "watch and pray" (see, for example, 1 Peter 4:7) so that we can always be alert and able to recognize the situations, people, relationships, jobs, and ministries that come into our life to form us. If Jesus had not discerned His processes through prayer, He never would have reached the cross. He might even have rebelled against the process. That means the resurrection would never have happened, because whoever does not die cannot be resurrected. But Jesus did not move an inch away from the center of God's will.

ONE OF THE SIGNS THAT A PERSON HAS BEEN PROCESSED IS THAT THEY ARE BROKEN AND DEAD TO SELF.

SUBMIT TO THE PROCESS VOLUNTARILY

I want to reemphasize that God does not force anyone to yield to Him. He does not violate our will. He frees us from all oppression so that we can freely choose Him. Submission to God's processes is therefore voluntary; it is something that everyone must decide for themselves. God calls us, urges us, attracts us, and waits for us, but the decision is ultimately ours. However, understand that if you say no to the process, you will never reach your destination or live in the fullness of your purpose.

Let's look at two biblical examples of leaders who willingly submitted to process: Joshua and Elisha. Joshua was a man of character who believed God's Word and promises, even when natural circumstances and events seemed to deny them. As a young man, he submitted himself to God's process by serving Moses; that is why, when Moses died, the mantle of leadership over the people of God was transferred to Joshua. *"Now Joshua the son of Nun was full of the spirit of wisdom, for Moses had laid his hands on him; so the children of Israel heeded him, and did as the LORD had commanded Moses"* (Deuteronomy 34:9). Joshua did not wait for God to tell him that he would be Moses's successor before he entered the process of submission. Joshua discerned his process years beforehand and voluntarily followed it in faith as God's will for his life.

Another example is that of Elisha. He submitted to the process of leaving his home and his family's wealth in order to voluntarily follow and serve the prophet Elijah. Nobody forced him to do this. Elijah called him, and Elisha followed him faithfully. That is why, when Elijah was taken up to heaven, Elisha received a double portion of his spirit. *"And so it was, when they had crossed over, that Elijah said to Elisha, 'Ask! What may I do for you, before I am taken away from you?' Elisha said, 'Please let a double portion of your spirit be upon me'"* (2 Kings 2:9). God granted Elisha's request, and Elisha had a powerful anointing. (See verses 10–15.)

We have all been created for a purpose—but not all of us fulfill it. There is an inescapable condition to our being formed for our destiny: surrender. Many people know their purpose, they know why God created them, but they are not willing to yield to the Lord. God will not force them. He works only with those who surrender their will to Him.

ACHIEVING SUCCESS IS NOT AS DIFFICULT AS SUSTAINING IT;
ONLY PROCESS CAN SUSTAIN IT.

Some people try to replace the process with prayer alone, not understanding that this is not the way either. Prayer helps us to discern the process and see more clearly which areas of our life we need to give over to God, and it gives us the strength to yield to Him, but it does not replace surrender.

If you want to discern and submit to your process, please say the following prayer with me:

> Heavenly Father, thank You for bringing all this knowledge about my purpose to me. It has allowed me to understand many of the situations that I have gone through in the past, as well as what I am going through today. Thank You for giving these circumstances of my life meaning!
>
> I acknowledge that I have not surrendered my will to You, and that I have fought against the process that can take me to my destiny. I ask You to forgive me for my ignorance and my rebellion. Today, I surrender my will to You, accepting You as the Lord of my life, and not only as my Savior. I give You the helm of my life and voluntarily submit to the process of being transformed and purified so that I can carry out my purpose in Your way.
>
> I trust in You and believe that everything You do in my life is for the purpose of leading me to true success. I declare that Christ is my role model, and that I will follow His

example of obedience and surrender. Today, I die to myself so that Christ may live fully in me, that His character may be formed in me, and that Your glorious purpose may be fulfilled in me. In the name of Jesus, amen!

TESTIMONIES OF FINDING AND FULFILLING PURPOSE

A REVELATION OF PURPOSE THROUGH SIGNS AND SERVICE

Lisandro Parra was a man who was lost in life, without direction or purpose, until he found Jesus. Today, he is a prophet in a church affiliated with King Jesus Ministry. This is his testimony:

> I came to know Christ in the darkest moment of my life. At that time, I was completely devoted to alcohol, cigarettes, and marijuana; I also used cocaine and was a womanizer. I lived from party to party. My world was a circle of "fun," drugs, and alcohol.
>
> I started this lifestyle when I was very young, and I did not know any different way of living. When I moved to Miami, things got even worse because drugs became more accessible to me. They were everywhere! I also led a very promiscuous life due to the example of my family. My grandfather was an adulterer, my father was an adulterer, and I followed the same pattern. At age twenty-four, I started hearing about God, but I did not surrender to Him. The woman I was with at the time spoke to me about God and took me to church, but I only went to please her. I received Christ, but not from the heart. However, from that day forward, I began to hear the voice of God, although I did not

THE GREATER THE ANOINTING, THE GREATER THE PROCESS. NO ONE CAN CARRY SOMETHING FOR WHICH THEY HAVE NOT BEEN PROCESSED.

commit myself to Him because the vices in my life had a strong grip on me.

Then, I started going through difficult situations that were like signs to me. It all began with a woman using Santeria witchcraft against me; then, somebody tried to take my life. After this, my business went bankrupt. Many times, I would wake up in the morning to find that I had crashed my car the night before while driving home under the influence of alcohol or drugs, but I was not hurt.

There came a time when I did not know what to do! I was looking for a solution but could not find it until I surrendered to God and made a covenant with Jesus. He freed me from prison and saved me from death, accidents, and much more. Today, I know it was all because of God's purpose in my life. During this time, I met the woman who would become my wife, and together we began to follow the ways of the Lord. The process God took me through was very hard; it involved radical changes. I was used to having a lot of money, and suddenly, I was left with nothing. I had always had everything, but now I found myself with barely enough financial resources. However, through all these changes, God was faithful.

When I started attending King Jesus Ministry, God began to reveal my purpose, little by little, through my acts of service. I started in the ministry of praise, and then I worked in the bookstore. After that, I moved to the ministry of intercession, where I served for several years. During this time, I was always available to help clean the bathrooms at the church, go out to evangelize, or serve in the school for new believers, in deliverance ministry, or in intercession. My wife and I did everything. God made us go us through the process. Through our service to others, and with the guidance of the Holy Spirit, we were built up and led to our purpose. This is how we developed in ministry and in life.

Today, we are living in our purpose. Recently, I was ordained as a prophet by our spiritual father, apostle Guillermo Maldonado, and I am the pastor of a King Jesus Ministry church in the city of Homestead, Florida. My wife and I feel fulfilled.

God is also using us in Medellin, Colombia, and in other parts of the world, building His people and raising men and women in their purposes. Through our ministry, we have seen God heal people from cancer and many other illnesses, restore marriages, and do much more. One man who was healed and restored was named Pedro. He had been using drugs for eleven years, and he did not want to know anything about God, but his wife prayed that he might know God's glory. One day, Pedro was diagnosed with seven herniated discs. As a result, he had to start taking a particular medication, but it caused a bad reaction. He felt desperate!

The doctors did not give Pedro hope because, in addition, alcoholism and smoking had caused serious damage to his body. We prayed for him and God did something radical in his life. From the first day that he arrived at the church, a process of change and healing began. God restored his health completely! His marriage was also restored.

THE END-TIME REMNANT WILL BE PROCESSED MORE THAN ANY OTHER GENERATION OF BELIEVERS.

Now, he and his wife are growing spiritually, and they are both deacons of the ministry. They are firm in serving and growing in God.

Pedro is finding his purpose as a leader in the church. He started studying the Bible, and many things in his life have changed. Because I found my purpose, others who have gone through the same thing I did are being transformed by the same God. We are very grateful for everything we have seen in our ministry, and for the lives that God has transformed around us.

I believe that the most complete happiness a human being can experience comes from being in the purpose and will of God. Living in my purpose, I feel peace, happiness, and joy, and I see its fruit in my life, in our home, in our church, and in my wife. God has blessed us in everything. Now I train the children of God in my church, even pastors from other countries, to lead them to their own purposes. We give glory to God for making everything possible and choosing us as servants of His kingdom, called to fulfill His purpose on earth!

THE SECRET TO DISCERNING THE PROCESSES THAT WILL LEAD US TO FULFILL OUR PURPOSE IS TO WATCH AND PRAY CONTINUALLY.

A BREAKTHROUGH TO A LIFE OF PURPOSE

After finding her purpose in God, Jacqueline Murphy of Miami, Florida, became a prolific writer and started five different companies in the publishing field.

> I always believed that God created me to be a unique person and that, one day, He would use all the talents and gifts He had given me. I also knew that God had a plan for me and that He would do great things in my life, but I had been looking for a place to start and had not yet found one.
>
> Then, I began to become interested in the supernatural power of God, and I connected with King Jesus Ministry. Ever since I was a little girl, I had enjoyed writing, but I had not published anything until I received an activation from God during a class at the University of the Supernatural Ministry (USM). I had arrived there with a manuscript for a book and a deep desire to show the world what God had given me. During one of the classes, I took that manuscript and, with all my faith, presented it to God.
>
> I had always felt great opposition and delay in my life. In fact, that manuscript had been sitting on a shelf for three years. In the beginning, I only had a vision of what God wanted me to do, although I knew that in my own strength I could not fulfill His plan. But

after I received the teaching at USM, my book was published, and I have been able to see the glory of God. In addition, God has helped me to start five different companies, all related to the publishing field.

Today, I am invited to many nations to talk about my experience in publishing. I have had crucial moments on my path, but God's plan has always prevailed. I have faced challenges, but now, after going through the process, I have been able to see my dream come true. All I needed was to learn to rest in God and believe in His purpose for my life.

ANOINTED FOR A PURPOSE

GOD WOULD NOT ENTRUST US WITH PURPOSE IF OUR SUBMISSION TO THE PROCESS WERE INVOLUNTARY.

4

ANOINTED FOR A PURPOSE

The generation that you and I belong to is influenced by a Western mentality that is based on rationalism, empirical science, and religious liberalism. Each of these approaches to life has a hard time recognizing and depending on God. In the last twenty years, we have seen major advances in the fields of medicine, technology, and science. Yet such advances have served to encourage weaknesses that are already present in our society's mind-set: we like to think we have everything under control, and we always want to solve every problem or issue instantly, in our own strength—through our knowledge, natural reasoning, and skills alone.

However, many serious problems persist in our society. The times we are living in have thrust complex circumstances upon us that are beyond our capacity to resolve. We see these challenges in all aspects of society, including government, economics, education, business, health, family, ministry, and many more. We have not recognized the fact that our original purpose as human beings does not come from the natural realm, even though we live in physical bodies and dwell in a material world. As we have affirmed throughout this book, we originated in God, and everything that comes from God has a supernatural beginning. We therefore need supernatural solutions to the issues in our own society and the problems we see throughout the earth.

Similarly, we cannot know or fulfill our true purpose in life with merely our natural abilities. Becoming who we were created to be is possible only through the grace, power, and anointing of God. Something that is supernatural is beyond the perception of our natural senses, and it transcends the boundaries of human reason and ability, as well as the limits of physical law. Thus, we categorically need the supernatural power God to fulfill His unique assignment for us on earth. It follows that if you believe you can achieve your purpose according to your own ability, it surely is not God's true purpose for you!

WHAT IS THE ANOINTING?

The supernatural power to carry out a purpose, call, or assignment from God is known as "the anointing." This is a theme we covered briefly in the last chapter when we talked about process, because only through God's process can we be prepared for His anointing. To "anoint" means to endow someone with divine ability to do what they could not do according to their own nature and gifts. To effectively fulfill the purpose God has given you, you must have the anointing of the Holy Spirit.

To be anointed is to be supernaturally empowered to do the impossible! Acts 10:38 says, "*God anointed Jesus of Nazareth with the Holy Spirit and*

> GOD WILL NOT GIVE A MANTLE OF SUCCESSION TO SOMEONE WHO DOES NOT WALK UNDER VOLUNTARY SUBJECTION.

with power, who went about doing good and healing all who were oppressed by the devil, for God was with Him." Are you facing something impossible? Are you trying to fulfill your purpose in your own strength? If your answer to either of these questions is yes, it is time to begin seeking the anointing of the Holy Spirit so you can receive God's supernatural strength and wisdom.

We always need to keep in mind that nothing God sends us to do is possible on our own. For example, Jesus has entrusted us with this mandate: "*And as you go, preach, saying, 'The kingdom of heaven is at hand.' Heal the sick, cleanse the lepers, raise the dead, cast out demons. Freely you have received, freely give*" (Matthew 10:7–8). This mandate can only be accomplished when we are anointed with power from on high. Therefore, Jesus explains, "*You shall receive power when the Holy Spirit has come upon you; and you shall be witnesses to Me in Jerusalem, and in all Judea and Samaria, and to the end of the earth*" (Acts 1:8).

KNOWING THE PURPOSE OF YOUR ANOINTING

The nature and measure of your anointing are given in accordance with your unique purpose. This divine ability is not given to you arbitrarily. It is not given to you with an option to use it or not. And it is not given to you merely for your own purposes. It is granted exclusively for the fulfillment of a specific purpose, call, or assignment. Whether that purpose is in the area of business, the arts, education, sports, technology, law, ministry, politics, government, science, medicine, or anything else, it can only be achieved in God. Therefore, no matter what sphere of influence or territory He has assigned to you, if you are working on the purpose He has given you, then you can be assured that God will provide you with His anointing.

Some people have divine ability, but they don't know the reason for which God has anointed them. Because they don't know how to connect their anointing with their purpose, they become extremely frustrated. Others don't even recognize that a divine anointing awaits them. This is one of the reasons why many people feel empty and unhappy. They are ineffective or unproductive in their lives because they are operating outside of their calling and purpose.

When Jesus began His ministry, He made it very clear what His purpose was and what He had been anointed for. Standing in the synagogue at Nazareth, He declared:

> *The Spirit of the Lord is upon Me, because He has anointed Me to preach the gospel to the poor; He has sent Me to heal the brokenhearted, to proclaim liberty to the captives and recovery of sight to the blind, to set at liberty those who are oppressed; to proclaim the acceptable year of the Lord.* (Luke 4:18–19)

Jesus was anointed for this very purpose! Now, my question to you is this: "Do you know what you have been anointed for?"

Jesus was able to demonstrate who He was, and what His purpose was, by means of the supernatural works produced by the anointing He carried. This anointing confirmed God's approval of His ministry. Peter said to the crowd at Pentecost, "*Men of Israel, hear these words: Jesus of Nazareth,* ***a Man attested by God*** *to you by miracles, wonders, and signs*

SURRENDER IS THE PLACE WHERE GOD BEGINS TO FORM US, AND THE TIME IT TAKES FOR US TO BE FORMED DEPENDS ON OUR LEVEL OF SURRENDER.

which God did through Him in your midst, as you yourselves also know..." (Acts 2:22).

In order to fulfill His purpose, Jesus not only needed to go through God's process of submission, but He also needed the approval of the Father. Jesus was perfect, holy, and pure, yet He had to be baptized in the Jordan River and fast for forty days in the desert before He could stand in the synagogue to read the first part of Isaiah 61 and then announce, "*Today this Scripture is fulfilled in your hearing*" (Luke 4:21). Nowadays, we have lowered the criteria of approval for serving in the ministry, so that the preaching of the gospel has often become a form of entertainment. Without a doubt, the true way to follow the will of God is the way that Jesus showed us. Now, ask yourself, "Does my life or ministry show evidence of having been approved by God?"

Today, in much of the church, we have replaced the anointing with education, natural abilities, gifts, and personal interests. In many cases, we no longer seek evidence of God's process and anointing on a person before ordaining them for ministry. Instead, we look more at titles and charisma. We conduct ourselves according to the way of the world and not in the manner of the kingdom. This practice is leading the church astray and is the reason why many Christian leaders and congregations are not being transformed, and therefore why they are not being effective or productive. Consequently, they are failing to impact their country and their generation. They may fill their agendas with congregational activities, but no supernatural change occurs.

To carry out our purpose and ministry without divine ability is to operate merely in "religion"—human formulas and methods, lifeless rituals, and so forth, "*having a form of godliness but denying its power*" (2 Timothy 3:5). The world is tired of religion, because religion lacks power. The church would achieve much more if it returned to the criteria established by Christ. We know that Jesus did not even begin His ministry until He was baptized in the Holy Spirit, or anointed. As a man, without the divine capacity He received at the Jordan River, He would not have been able to heal the sick, cast out demons, raise the dead, or preach the good news of the kingdom. He would not have been able to achieve the results He obtained in accordance with His purpose.

God will always confirm our purpose, call, or assignment with a supernatural intervention, such as a prophetic word, a dream, a vision, a sign, or another divine communication. He will make this confirmation very clear to us, so that it is not something we can easily overlook or fail to recognize. It is a moment that marks us, changes us, and remains engraved in our memory and in our hearts. If you have not had such a moment in your life, you have not yet entered into your anointing to fulfill your purpose. It could be that you have not submitted to God's process or are still in the midst of that process.

IS SOMETHING HINDERING YOUR ANOINTING?

Although God will clarify His will for us, many people still ask, "How can I recognize that God's anointing has come to me for a purpose?" To recognize that moment, it is important to know that the anointing comes to empower us to fulfill *a specific assignment*. Remember that the anointing does not come just to make us feel good or even so that we will feel the presence of God—although His presence accompanies the anointing.

GOD IS A SUPERNATURAL BEING, WITH SUPERNATURAL ABILITIES, WHOSE PURPOSES ARE ALSO SUPERNATURAL.

Sometimes, the anointing does not appear to come because we lack expectation about what God wants to do through our lives; we can't imagine receiving the type of assignment He wants to give us. Therefore, we need to be aware that God always wants to do a special work in us. All that He requires is that we be available. Jesus said, *"Blessed are the poor in spirit, for theirs is the kingdom of heaven. Blessed are those who mourn, for they shall be comforted. Blessed are the meek, for they shall inherit the earth. Blessed are those who hunger and thirst for righteousness, for they shall be filled"* (Matthew 5:3–6). If you humbly seek the Lord and obey His Word, He will reveal your purpose and assignment, and your anointing will be activated.

Other times, people will try to serve God, and then they wonder why the anointing does not come. The anointing will not accompany us when we are attempting to do something that is not part of our assignment, because then we are not aligned with God's purpose. Under such conditions, people often burn themselves out because they do not have the grace to carry out that assignment. The anointing comes to set you apart and empower you to serve the Lord according to the purpose for which He created you.

Another way the divine empowerment can be blocked is when we are self-centered, not acknowledging that our purpose isn't just about ourselves, but about serving others. Although God has a personal or specific plan for your life, He doesn't work with you in an isolated way. He always views you as a member of His people, His family, not as an individual separate from others. If you are trying to fulfill a purpose that only benefits you, then the anointing of God will not follow.

We are consecrated and anointed for a specific purpose. However, the moment we leave that purpose, the anointing stops working because it is not given to us to do whatever we want with it. On the other hand, when we are operating in our purpose, the anointing produces fruit and multiplication; everything flows, and we feel "tailored" for exactly what we are doing.

So, when is the anointing given or activated? When we know our purpose. And what is it for? To fulfill the purpose for which God created us. Once we know our purpose and assignment, God expects us to respond to His call. There is an interval between being anointed and being sent out. During that time, God expects a yes from us to fulfill His purpose. Are you willing to say yes to God?

THE PLACE OF ANOINTING

Many people also wonder *where* they will be anointed, or empowered. They ask, "Do I need to be in a church?" "Should I ask a pastor to anoint me with oil?" or "Do I have to wait somewhere for an angel to come with a message from God?" There really is no specific physical place you need to be to receive God's anointing. However, there *is* a place in the Spirit where you must be.

We read in the Gospels that Jesus went down to the Jordan River to be baptized, at which time He was anointed. Here is the description of this event from the book of Luke: "*When all the people were baptized, it came to pass that Jesus also was baptized; and while He prayed, the heaven was opened. And the Holy Spirit descended in bodily form like a dove upon Him*" (Luke 3:21–22). Spiritually speaking, the Jordan represents a place of surrender, where we submit our will to God's will and accept God's way over our way. This

EVERYTHING JESUS COMMISSIONED US TO DO IS IMPOSSIBLE TO ACHIEVE IN THE NATURAL.

is the place of death to ourselves that we talked about earlier. When Jesus was baptized in the Jordan, it was an unequivocal sign that He was surrendering His will to the Father and was ready to be anointed.

In the Old Testament, there is an account of a Syrian army general named Naaman who was suffering from leprosy. He went to Israel looking for the prophet Elisha because he knew that God had used him to do miracles. However, when Naaman arrived, the prophet did not even go out to meet him. Instead, he gave this order by means of a messenger: *"Go and wash in the Jordan seven times, and your flesh shall be restored to you, and you shall be clean"* (2 Kings 5:10).

The Jordan was a river of dirty water, so the general was offended by that instruction. He would have preferred to have washed in a river in his own country, like the Abanah, which had cleaner water. Naaman almost refused God's prescription for healing, until his servants persuaded him to obey this simple task. The Bible says, *"So he went down and dipped seven times in the Jordan, according to the saying of the man of God; and his flesh was restored like the flesh of a little child, and he was clean"* (2 Kings 5:14).

Naaman needed to humble himself and be cleansed in God's way in order to be healed. This teaches us that, to follow God, we have to walk according to the route of surrender and humility. Walking according to the path of the world—with our skill, talent, education, and human wisdom—is not enough. These elements might work when it comes to doing a natural job, but they are not sufficient for performing a supernatural assignment. The only legal way to receive God's anointing, or divine ability, is to die to yourself, deny the flesh, and yield to His will. Jesus always walked in the anointing because He continually lived a life of surrender. He died to His own will in order to do the Father's will (see, for example, Luke 22:42), and He humbled Himself to allow the anointing to flow through Him.

THE ANOINTING DEMONSTRATES GOD'S APPROVAL OF YOUR PURPOSE.

RECEIVING YOUR ANOINTING

It is God's will that we live under the anointing of the Holy Spirit in order to accomplish our purpose and calling. The only place from which we can minister to others is this place of anointing. We have to choose the way of God because only then will we be empowered to bring His kingdom to earth through our assignment.

To conclude, we can say that anointing is the grace and supernatural power of God that enables us to fulfill the purpose or call that the Lord has given us. The anointing is granted exclusively to fulfill a divine assignment that separates and consecrates us for a specific mission in life. In addition, the anointing is proof that we are operating in the right calling. It comes to us in that place where we surrender our will to the will of the Father.

Have you received an anointing from God? Have you undergone the process of being formed so that you can know your purpose and correctly apply your anointing? Today, once again, the challenge is to surrender completely to God so that He can fulfill His plans in your life, and the anointing of the Holy Spirit can empower you to achieve the impossible for the kingdom.

Let's pray together so that the divine anointing can flow in your life and you can fulfill the true purpose for which you were created.

Heavenly Father, I thank You for the revelation that You have provided through this chapter. Thank You for giving me everything I need to be able to fulfill Your will in my life. I recognize that, for a long time, I have tried to do things my own way, according to my natural strengths and abilities. Now I understand why many things have not worked out for me, and why it always seems as if I am missing something. I confess that I have lacked the faith to believe that You want to do great things through my life. I have also neglected to surrender completely to You. Today, I voluntarily renounce my efforts to achieve a divine purpose according to my natural abilities. I yield my will, I surrender my life, and I die to myself so that Your anointing can empower me to achieve my true purpose on earth. I will give You all the glory, in public and in private. In the mighty name of Jesus, amen!

TESTIMONIES OF FINDING AND FULFILLING PURPOSE

ANOINTED TO HEAL AND RESUSCITATE

Lizthsol is a Mexican nurse who received the revelation of her purpose and surrendered her life to be empowered by divine skill in order to fulfill her destiny in the field of surgery.

> I have seen God do extraordinary things, not only in my career, but also in my personal life. The Lord revealed His glory when I had a very difficult pregnancy. Before I became pregnant, I told God that, when I had a baby, whether it was a boy or a girl, I would give the baby to Him to serve Him. I did not know anything about making covenants with God, but this pledge came out of my heart.
>
> When I became pregnant, there were medical complications, and the doctors said the baby might need to be aborted, but I made it through the first two trimesters. Then, in my third trimester, I was diagnosed with preeclampsia. As a result, the baby had to be born prematurely. He was hospitalized, and he required constant monitoring. After he was released from the hospital, over time, I noticed that he frequently became sick. I asked God why He would let my child get sick if I had offered him up to Him. After the baby was one year old, he started to have a constant fever. My husband is a doctor, so

THE SCRIPTURAL CRITERION FOR SERVING IN THE MINISTRY HAS ALWAYS BEEN TO BE ANOINTED WITH DIVINE CAPACITY.

he began to do tests, but he said he didn't find anything alarming. However, one day, when I got home from work, I saw that our son again had a fever. I did not even know how to pray, but I asked God to heal him. Suddenly, he had a seizure that lasted almost fifteen minutes.

Desperate, I rushed him to the hospital, arrived at the emergency area, and gave him to my husband to be checked. They knew he had an infection, but they did not know where it was located in his body, so they did a lot of tests. They could not find the cause until they performed a lumbar puncture; then, they found that the problem was viral meningitis. The worse my son's condition grew, the more bitter I became toward God. As the days passed, even though my child began to improve, he suffered aftereffects of recurrent seizures.

Months later, I went to visit my mother in another city, and a friend contacted me and told me she was praying for me. She attended a church in Miami called King Jesus Ministry, and she told us about the miracles that God does there. She also told me about God's purpose for my life and my family. Upon hearing all of this, my sister was encouraged to visit the church. She came back completely different! So, that same year, I decided to go too.

Right before my husband and I took our son to King Jesus Ministry, we had him tested, and we scheduled an assessment appointment with a pediatric neurologist. She told us that his brain had been affected in the area of learning and that he was mentally retarded. The doctor prescribed medication, which she said our son needed to take until he turned fifteen. I did not accept that diagnosis!

During one of the conferences sponsored by King Jesus Ministries, we received the impartation of healing, and we believed that God had acted. Later that year, we brought my son back to have a repeat of the test that had diagnosed his mental retardation. The test results were excellent, as if he had never had mental retardation! His brain looked completely normal. God did something that science could not do. Then, I understood that I had to go through all of that so that I would approach the Father, cling to Him, and fulfill His purpose for our lives.

Today, my son is nine years old and is a very intelligent child. He has never relapsed or suffered a seizure again. The power of God has no limits! We are happy and expectant of what God will do with his life.

I am a surgical nurse in a hospital in Mexico, and God has put a passion in me to help people. I know that He uses me there with purpose. I have had many situations where only the anointing of God could have done the miracle that saved a person's life. Let me tell you about a particular case. I was working my shift when the staff was suddenly informed that a person with a knife wound was coming in. People know me in my work, not only as a nurse but also as a woman of faith. The moment the patient entered the surgical room, the doctors declared him

ANOINTING IS THE DIVINE ABILITY THAT CONFIRMS OUR PURPOSE AND CALLING AND EMPOWERS US TO FULFILL IT.

dead. Instantly, everyone turned their eyes to me, and one of them told me, "Liz, start praying, because we have to get him out of here alive." I began to pray and declare the power of the resurrection over him. I cried out to God, declaring that when He did that miracle and everyone saw His glory, they would testify of the immensity of His power. While I was still praying, signs of life began to appear in the patient. After this, the doctors were able to perform surgery and save his life. The resurrection exists! As believers, we can be used to raise the dead!

I have attended the Supernatural Ministry School (SMS) at King Jesus, and God has empowered and equipped me to fulfill my purpose in medicine. He has edified me in creative miracles and taken my faith to another level; thus, I have been able to see my purpose develop in another dimension.

FROM BUDDHIST TO CHRISTIAN ENTREPRENEUR AND EVANGELIST

During our first Supernatural Encounter in Taiwan, we were received by the hungriest people of God that I have ever known. As soon as I entered the place where the meeting was being held, I felt a wave of expectation. In that atmosphere, I preached about God being above the laws of nature, science, and sickness. Then, I ministered to the crowd with what He had put in my heart. The Lord had told me in prayer, "I want to create organs in their bodies." So, we started praying for people, and, suddenly, creative miracles began to happen. For example, a woman named Cathy told us that she had been diagnosed with breast cancer eight years earlier, and 30 percent of her left breast had been removed. While we were praying, she began to feel warmth in that area of her body, and when she checked herself, she saw that her breast had regrown to its normal size, as if nothing had ever been removed! God is doing wonderful things in Taiwan and fulfilling great purposes.

Among those attending that meeting was an entrepreneur named Tony Tseng, who was introduced to me by Apostle Mike Connell. Tony leads a tremendous ministry in Taiwan. This is his testimony:

> My parents were Buddhists, so I did not know God or the plans He had for me. When it came time to choose a vocation, I decided on business because I was an ambitious young man. My first job was with one of the largest American companies in

THE ANOINTING WILL COME INTO YOUR LIFE WHEN YOU FIND YOUR PURPOSE AND WILL INCREASE AS YOU REMAIN THERE.

Taiwan. I quickly made a career for myself, and my future looked promising.

Even so, I did not feel satisfied inside. I was a perfectionist, and nobody could reach my standards. That made me feel empty and disappointed. Then, I met a coworker who guided me to Christ, and my life took a 180-degree turn. My values, lifestyle, and preferences changed completely. The business world began to bore me. Previously, morality had not mattered to me; the only thing that had been important to me was money, but this had only attracted worldly pleasures and more temptations. Now, everything that I had previously enjoyed and longed for no longer appealed to me. I was willing to leave everything for Christ.

My heart wanted to serve God full-time in the ministry, but the Lord did not allow me to. Instead, He gave me a word of revelation to stay in business. That word disturbed me a lot, and I struggled with this idea for a while. I asked God to speak to me again if He wanted me to remain in the business world. He answered me with a word from Psalm 42:11 and Psalm 43:5. I knew in my heart that God had answered my prayer, and I stayed in the field of finance. Then, I asked the Lord to guide me to a new job at another company, since I wanted a change of environment. I ended up in a small German firm, where I faced problems with the unwritten laws of the business world. But there I also learned to follow Christ and cling to my faith in the midst of conflicts.

I learned to put my career on the cross of Christ, because I had to reject tempting job offers with high profits to obey the voice of the Holy Spirit. Then, when the manager of my company was relocated to Germany, he chose me to replace him. Managing and expanding a small firm is the best way to gain experience,

NO ONE IS ANOINTED BY CHANCE;
THE ANOINTING SERVES A SPECIFIC PURPOSE.

and under my leadership, the company doubled its size several times. God arranged that training plan for me in order to equip me to serve in His kingdom, which was the job I had been asking for the whole time.

As I matured in the field of business, God gave me the vision to "build a glorious church," and I began to serve in my church in whatever area I was given the opportunity. I even served as chairman of the church council for more than thirty years. My church, Bread of Life, has grown from a few hundred people to more than ten thousand members, with over two hundred branches in Taiwan and a network of four hundred churches around the world.

God also gave me the vision to bring men to Christ and lead businessmen to serve Him. I believe that the gospel has two purposes: personal salvation and social transformation. With these ideas in mind, I founded an organization to minister to entrepreneurs, which has been leading businessmen to Christ for over thirty years and igniting their passion for serving God.

However, I still felt a pain inside me. A passion for the kingdom of God was still burning in my heart. I wanted to see the gospel preached everywhere and my country transformed. One day, the Holy Spirit led me to cry out in prayer in the presence of God. I felt that my abilities were limited and that I could not do more. But, after that time of prayer, God assured me that He would multiply the resources He had already provided for me.

In 1997, the Lord gave me a vision for a media ministry, and I began to feel a great burden to start a Christian television station. Building and operating a TV station is not cheap, and my business friends did not think it was a good idea. However, under the guidance of the Holy Spirit, I decided to build GOOD TV. We have been operating the station for more than twenty years, supported by donations and offerings from the audience. We have modernized, and now we make the message of the gospel available to Chinese peoples around the world through cable TV, satellite, and the Internet. In these twenty-plus years, the percentage of Christians in Taiwan has gone from 3 percent to 7 percent. I give glory to God for the small portion of responsibility that GOOD TV has had in this great harvest.

PURPOSE, TIMES, AND SEASONS

SURRENDER IS THE PLACE WHERE WE ARE EMPOWERED WITH DIVINE ABILITIES.

5

PURPOSE, TIMES, AND SEASONS

After we are anointed for our specific assignment, we must learn to recognize the season or seasons God sends us for fulfilling the purpose for which we were created. Remember, God dwells in a dimension called eternity that is beyond the cycle of natural life on earth and is not subject to the limitations of time. There is no past or future in eternity; instead, everything exists in an *eternal present*. Eternity *has always been*, *is*, and *will be*. In contrast, everything on earth is subject to time, in which there is past, present, and future, and by which our natural lives are governed.

The physical seasons are caused by the tilt of the earth's axis and the passage of time as our planet orbits around the sun. Spring, summer, autumn, and winter each make their own yearly appearance. Similarly, in the spiritual realm, there are unique seasons, or periods, when God brings about change to further His purposes for humanity. However, unlike the designated three-month seasons on the calendar, spiritual seasons vary in length—they might be short or long. Most of us experience multiple spiritual seasons in life as God works out His plans through us.

In the book of Ecclesiastes, King Solomon describes the cycles of life in the dimension of our earth, saying, "*To everything there is a season, a time for every purpose under heaven"* (Ecclesiastes 3:1). There are three key words in this verse that I use to explain how God unfolds our spiritual calling: *"season," "time,"* and *"purpose."* Understanding the relationship between these elements, as well as their differences, will help you to better grasp how they function in God's plan for your life. We will explore the words in reverse order: *purpose, time,* and *season.*

TO MOVE IN DIVINE ABILITY, WE MUST BE UNDER THE CONTROL, INFLUENCE, AND AUTHORITY OF GOD.

PURPOSE

Let's begin by reviewing the definition of "purpose," because it is important for understanding God's plans for us in connection with times and seasons: *purpose is the original intent for which someone or something was created.* Those who don't know their purpose will not be ready for their seasons. In fact, you have to know your purpose to be entitled to enter into the corresponding seasons for fulfilling it. Therefore, we can conclude that knowing and following your purpose guarantees that you will receive your seasons. When someone is aligned with their purpose, their seasons are assured.

TIME

"Time" refers to the number of days that God gives us to live on the earth. It belongs purely in the natural realm because time is a temporary entity. The Bible says that the former things will pass away. (See Revelation 21:4.)

For many people in our fallen world, time is just an interval in which they breathe, eat, sleep, and work. They pass their days without hope and without purpose. In prison terminology, there is an expression that is used to describe the period when a prisoner must remain incarcerated, away from public life, as a punishment for their crime. It is called "doing time" or "serving time." Prisoners are locked up for a designated period, which may be months or years. As they pay the penalty for their offenses, those who are incarcerated usually feel as if they are wasting their time, not doing anything constructive, not pursuing a purpose. There is a similar effect on a spiritual level. When we have no purpose in life, we are merely "serving time," allowing each day that we are given on earth to pass by without our doing anything purposeful or having anything special happen to us. This is a burdensome existence. However, for those who know their purpose, their time on earth has meaning because it is the period in which they go through the processes of learning and growing that lead them to fulfill that purpose.

SEASON

A spiritual season is a period of days, months, or years that is distinct in itself, but also joins with other periods to form a set of seasons related to one's purpose. It is a period marked by divine favor and supernatural events—a stage of peace, joy, blessings, abundance, grace, anointing, faith, and love.

We need to recognize how time and seasons are distinct. While time is related to the natural world, seasons are marked by supernatural activity. While time is temporary, seasons are given by the everlasting Father to move us toward a purpose that has eternal ramifications. When someone does not know their purpose, they cannot experience supernatural seasons. This is why their life on earth feels like a prison sentence.

We can learn to recognize the spiritual seasons in our lives, which we identify by divine signs, much as we identify seasons in the natural realm. Although weather patterns in the physical world do not always follow the seasons as indicated by the calendar, they are the most common way in which we recognize a particular season, especially in certain regions of the world. When the leaves on the trees start turning colors and falling to the ground, we know that autumn is here. When the temperature drops to its lowest range, we know that we have entered the season of winter. When the trees and flowers begin to bloom again and flocks of birds return from their migration, we know that spring is here. When the temperature rises to its highest range, we know that summer has come. Later in this chapter, we will talk more about identifying the seasons in our lives.

MAKING THE MOST OF YOUR SEASON

It is during a God-given season that we can accomplish what He has called us to do during that period—not beforehand or afterward. We can understand this concept from some simple examples related to the natural world. If you are a student in a degree program at a university, then you must make the most of your four years at that institution, gleaning all you can during this concentrated time of learning, because after you graduate, you will go on to other endeavors, and you won't have the same opportunities to devote yourself to study. If you are a parent, then you have about eighteen years to raise your children in the ways of the Lord. After that, they will be on their own, and you will not have the same influence in their lives. In the realm of government, someone who is elected president of the United States has a season of only four years—or eight, if they are reelected—to accomplish their goals and perhaps change the course of the nation.

In previous chapters, we have looked at the lives of Moses and Jesus as our primary biblical examples of the way God uses process in our lives to lead us to our purpose. After Moses's birth, he spent a period of forty years in Egypt. Then, he was processed for forty more years while he served as a shepherd in Midian, tending the flocks of his father-in-law, Jethro. This was a time of self-assessment and humility for him. When Moses's primary season arrived, he was eighty years old. At that point, he returned to Egypt to free the people of God through powerful miracles and lead them through the desert for another forty years.

Jesus was processed for thirty years before His season of ministry, which lasted three-and-a-half years. We have very little information about what Jesus's life was like before His ministry began. In those thirty years, He led a quiet life, out of the public eye. He spent much of His time helping His natural father, Joseph, with their carpentry business. During that period, nothing extraordinary happened in His life, but it was a time of personal and spiritual growth and faithful obedience to His heavenly Father. Then, as we know, at age thirty, Jesus was baptized by John in the Jordan River, and from that moment, He started His public life. His season was marked by miracles, signs, and wonders. In only three-and-a-half years, Jesus changed the history of humanity.

To be successful, to make our mark in society, and to change the world, we need be in a divine season. There are people who are more anointed, more educated, more intelligent, more skilled, more talented, and more capable than others, but because they have not yet entered their season, they are not able to completely fulfill their purpose or move to the next stage of that purpose. However, others who are less anointed and talented may be in the prime of their divine season, achieving great things linked to their purpose. They are in demand because they currently have special favor from God. Again, purpose is not as much about our ability as it is our availability and the timing of God's seasons for us.

I have gone through various seasons in my life. Right now, I am in a new season because God has given me a new mantle, with greater power and authority. As a result, I have seen an explosive increase of the supernatural in my ministry. Upon receiving this new cloak, I entered a fresh season in which "mega-miracles"—bigger and larger supernatural manifestations, which have exceeded all expectations—are what prevail.

When God visited me and granted me that new mantle, He told me that its purpose was to give me access to people, places, and things that I had not had before. Today, I am obtaining more and more influence with people in the highest spheres of politics in the United States, and more influence in other countries. If I have been able to enter a new season and walk in the influence and power that come with it, then you can too. The requirement is to commit to doing God's will rather than pursue your own agenda.

PRINCIPLES FOR PURPOSE AND SEASONS

The following are some essential principles related to purpose and seasons that we must bear in mind.

PEOPLE WITHOUT PURPOSE LIVE AS PRISONERS OF TIME, WHICH IS A BURDENSOME EXISTENCE.

SEASONS ARE GIVEN ACCORDING TO PURPOSE

Every season begins with the revelation of origin and purpose. If you do not know where you came from, then you will not know the purpose of your life or where you are going, and you will not receive your season. We are not the product of astral explosions or the evolutionary process. Our origin is in God. We are divine creations; our heavenly Father formed us with His own hands, and He planned our purpose from the beginning.

> *Then God said, "Let Us make man in Our image, according to Our likeness; let them have dominion over the fish of the sea, over the birds of the air, and over the cattle, over all the earth and over every creeping thing that creeps on the earth." So God created man in His own image; in the image of God He created him; male and female He created them. Then God blessed them, and God said to them, "Be fruitful and multiply; fill the earth and subdue it; have dominion over the fish of the sea, over the birds of the air, and over every living thing that moves on the earth."* (Genesis 1:26–28)

Remember that as we go through God's processes, we begin to identify our individual purpose. Where there is no purpose, there can be no season of supernatural manifestation and blessing. Only the knowledge of purpose attracts the supernatural, opens the heavens, and causes the Holy Spirit to pour out His anointing. I can't emphasize enough that we must know the purpose that God has given to our life. Otherwise, we will merely bide our time, feeling tired and bored, having nothing new happen to us and making no advancements.

Moreover, if we are unclear about our purpose, we will not recognize when a season comes to us or understand what that season is to be used for. When this happens, we miss valuable opportunities. There are people who boast, "This is my season," but they do not really understand the meaning of that season, and they end up losing out. Purpose and seasons are not about feeling certain emotions or even reciting particular faith declarations. They are about revelation that comes as a consequence of a relationship with God that is established by knowing our origin in Him.

PURPOSE IS REGULATED BY SEASONS

The reason God established seasons in the natural world was to give balance and order to creation. Human beings were designed to experience change from one earthly season to another. Similarly, we are designed to move from one spiritual season to another, always in fulfillment of our purpose. Merely "doing time" doesn't have to be our only option in life. If we remain in our purpose and learn to discern the seasons of God's grace and favor, we will accomplish great feats. (See Psalm 108:13.)

SEASONS ARE EITHER SOVEREIGN OR STIRRED UP

Some seasons come into our lives purely by the sovereign choice of God. However, the Lord also gives us the opportunity to stir seasons up. If you want to provoke a season, then plant a seed—invest in some way in God's kingdom—and stay on the lookout. (See, for example, Luke 6:38.) The seasons will come to you, but again, if you do not take advantage of them, you risk aborting them or losing them.

ONLY GOD KNOWS WHEN OUR SEASON WILL BEGIN OR HOW LONG IT WILL LAST, BUT WE CAN PREPARE FOR IT THROUGH DEVOTION TO HIM AND OBEDIENCE TO HIS WORD.

SOME SEASONS ARE PROMPTED BY EXTERNAL PROVOCATION

Most people prefer to live in their comfort zone. Only a few dare to go out and take action, even when provoked. For example, the Bible shows us that although David loved God, the little shepherd boy did not stop looking after sheep—his comfort zone—until he was provoked by the Philistine giant, Goliath, who challenged the army of the Lord. That provocation was what awakened the king inside David. Let me ask you, "What or who is provoking you? Will that provocation awaken your purpose, or will you just keep 'doing time'"?

A CHANGING SEASON BRINGS NEW CONNECTIONS

In my own life, I have noticed that my season changes after I meet certain people whom God has put in my life. These are people who have specific qualifications or gifts from God that help boost the effectiveness and reach of my ministry. After each new connection, I see increased blessing, favor, revelation, faith, anointing, and prosperity. What happened for me will also happen for you. God is bringing someone into your life in connection with a new season that will change the way you live. You must be prepared to discern, or recognize, that person or persons.

ALL SEASONS MUST BE DISCERNED

In order to recognize a season, we need the discernment of the Holy Spirit. That is why it is so important to have an intimate relationship with God. His Spirit can open our spiritual eyes to see and recognize the seasons that the Father sends into our life. We cannot recognize them with our natural senses. Unless we sharpen our spiritual senses, we may hesitate when presented with a divine opportunity and let the season pass. Or, we may become distracted by situations that, although they seem to come from God, will lead us down blind alleys.

There is a saying, "To each his own," which refers to a person's individual preferences, tastes, and interests. In a spiritual sense, we could say that "to each his own" represents an individual's purpose, calling, and assignment—that for which they are known, or will ultimately be known. "Your own" is your niche in the market, the skill at which you excel, the area in which you are an expert, and so forth. It is essential that you learn to discern what is "your own" as you go through the process of discovering and preparing for your purpose.

Adam's purpose was to be the first man to rule the world. Noah's calling was to obediently build an ark to preserve the human race in the great flood, even though it had never before rained on the earth. Joseph's mission was to be Egypt's "prime minister" and preserve the lineage of the Messiah during a time of dire famine. Moses's purpose was to be the leader and liberator of the people of Israel. King David's calling was to be a worshipper whose heart was pleasing to God, and to be a warrior who would fight Israel's battles. John the Baptist's mission was to prepare the way for the Messiah. Mary's calling was to give birth to God's Son, *"the firstborn over all creation"* (Colossians 1:15), the Savior of the world. Jesus's purpose was to pay the price of our redemption and restore humanity to the presence of the Father. The apostle Paul's directive was to preach the gospel of the kingdom to the Gentiles. My own calling is to bring the supernatural power of God to this

IF WE HAVE NOT YET ENTERED OUR SEASON,
WE CANNOT FULFILL OUR PURPOSE.

generation—to be an apostle to the world, approved by God with the manifestations of miracles, signs, and wonders.

What is your purpose? What is the reason for your existence? If you are tired of merely existing on this earth, prepare to enter your season.

SEASONS BEGIN WITH OPPORTUNITY AND REQUIRE COMMITMENT

When we enter a God-given season, opportunities will present themselves in the form of places, things, or people. I like to call these "divine connections." Then, after an opportunity presents itself, we have to make an investment in it. In the Bible, a rich young man asked Jesus what he needed to do to inherit eternal life. However, he did not want to make the investment that Jesus demanded—to sell all his possessions and follow Jesus—and he missed the opportunity that was offered to him. (See, for example, Matthew 19:16–22.) In contrast, Jesus's disciples left everything to follow their Master. Jesus Himself invested everything He had to fulfill His purpose. He gave His own life to gain access to His best season—as the resurrected Savior who has redeemed humanity to God and who is King of Kings and Lord of Lords, with all authority in heaven and on earth. (See Matthew 28:18.) In the eyes of God, if we do not make an investment in our purpose, we show that we are not committed to it. When God gives you an opportunity to enter your season, invest in it!

WE MUST BE PREPARED AND CONDITIONED FOR A NEW SEASON

How do we prepare for a season? It is very similar to how we prepare for the natural seasons and opportunities of life. When winter approaches, we put away our light clothes and take out our warm clothes. We might buy new boots or a new coat. When a season of competition approaches, athletes begin a rigorous program to improve their physical conditioning. When college students anticipate a new term, they sign up for courses and purchase books and perhaps a new laptop. When a couple is about to get married, they prepare for their new household by looking for an apartment or house, sending invitations to those with whom they want to share their special day, and going to premarital counseling. When baseball season approaches, fans begin talking about the prospects of their favorite team and what new players have come on the scene, and purchase tickets to the games they plan to attend.

Knowing that God will be sending us a supernatural season, we must be spiritually prepared for it. We need to realize that before taking us to the season in which we will fulfill our purpose, God transforms our heart and shapes our character. When our heart is transformed, we are ready for that new season. We can cooperate in this process by developing and strengthening our spiritual life through prayer, fasting, reading the Word, seeking God's face, surrendering to His will, forgiving and receiving forgiveness, purifying our heart, making covenants with God, learning from solid Bible teachers who can aid our spiritual development, and building helpful mentorships and friendships, while letting go of harmful relationships.

We can also prepare for a new season mentally and emotionally. For example, if God wants to take you into a season of financial expansion, you need to have gained a certain degree of knowledge in the area of finances and have the experience to handle a large contract. Whatever your purpose, you must be

WHEN YOU DO NOT KNOW YOUR PURPOSE,
YOU DO NOT QUALIFY FOR A SEASON.

prepared for a new season—to expand your business, to receive a job promotion, to have your marriage restored, to reestablish a relationship with your children, to enter a new or expanded direction for your ministry, and so on. Most people do not prepare; therefore, they are not in a spiritual, emotional, mental, or physical state to enter the new season that awaits them.

THE BEGINNING AND END OF EACH SEASON WILL BE MARKED BY TESTS

If you have been tested, pressed, and stretched, it is a sign that you are about to enter a new season in life. These tests are the door to the next season for fulfilling your purpose. Or, they might mean that a particular season is ending, and you are being tried regarding what you have learned during that time and if your faith and trust in God will hold steady under increased pressure.

> *I know that whatever God does, it shall be forever. Nothing can be added to it, and nothing taken from it. God does it, that men should fear before Him. That which is has already been, and what is to be has already been; and God requires an account of what is past.*
> (Ecclesiastes 3:14–15)

We must serve God faithfully during our season, making good use of that time. This will show Him that we are able to handle an extended season or another new season.

THE PURPOSE GUARANTEES THE SEASON

If you are in your purpose, your season is guaranteed. You only have to enter it by faith and begin to walk in the supernatural, accomplishing the plan that God has designed for your life on earth. Although the purpose may seem impossible to fulfill, you should not fear, because each purpose is guaranteed the seasons that will make possible its fulfillment.

WHEN WE ARE IN OUR SEASON, WE ENTER INTO DEMAND BECAUSE GOD MAKES EVERY SEED WE SOW MOVE IN OUR FAVOR.

If you want God to send a supernatural season in which you can see miracles, signs, wonders, and His plans for your life unfold, you need to surrender yourself to Him completely and position yourself by preparing your heart and mind. Only then will your marriage, your children, your ministry, your job or business, your finances, your church, and your city come into harmony with the purpose He has given you.

The following prayer will guide you in this process. Please pray it out loud and from your heart:

> Heavenly Father, I thank You for the revelation I have received in this chapter. I understand that I must discern and make use of the seasons You give me, which will enable me to fulfill my calling. I know that I have not always recognized the testing that comes with a new season in my life and have resisted going through it, which has blocked my progress in achieving the purpose You have planned for me. Today, I ask for Your forgiveness, and I cry out for a new opportunity. Lord, I will die to myself and submit to Your process, because I know a new season is coming. I promise to prepare and condition myself to receive what You want to give me. I commit myself, under the guidance of the Holy Spirit, to make room for new seasons. With all my heart, I ask You not to allow me to continue to miss opportunities that come from You. Help me to discern and make use

of every resource, gift, and person You bring into my life, so I may enter into new seasons and live in the supernatural power of my purpose. I no longer want to just "serve time." I want to enter into Your eternal realm, where divine ability will enable me to extend Your kingdom on earth and leave a legacy of Your life, transformation, and power in this world. I pray this in the mighty name of Jesus. Amen!

OUR FIDELITY TO A SEASON WILL DETERMINE WHETHER GOD WILL RENEW IT.

TESTIMONIES OF FINDING AND FULFILLING PURPOSE

FROM STRUGGLING PASTOR TO COSTA RICAN CONGRESSMAN

When Pastor Harllan Hoepelman Páez, from Costa Rica, connected with our ministry, he began to enter into his season. The supernatural power of God was released in his life, his ability to fulfill his purpose was strengthened, and God's promises began to be fulfilled at all levels. Today, he is a man of God with great influence in the politics of his country.

> My name is Harllan Hoepelman Páez, and I lead a congregation in Costa Rica, which we started nine years ago, practically alone, guided by a dream of God. Although we faced multiple obstacles, we were overcoming them one by one. When we connected with King Jesus Ministry, we experienced great growth. First, I read Apostle Maldonado's book *The Glory of God,* and sometime later, I read *How to Walk in the Supernatural Power of God.* I began to disciple the members of the church with this material. At that time, there were five hundred members; today, there are two thousand.
>
> Before connecting with King Jesus Ministry, I had been about to close the church due to a number of setbacks, which prevented us from having a building of our own. However, God opened a door for us in a supernatural

way, and we obtained a lot located on a main street, with enough space to build a church that included all the amenities we had yearned for.

After construction was complete, we faced new obstacles due to the dizzying growth of our youth group. We became a nuisance to the neighbors. The Ministry of Health and the municipality closed the premises several times. The situation generated a constant clash with the authorities of the city. We had to request meetings with governmental representatives, starting with the mayor of the district, the health authorities, and even some deputies (legislators) of the Republic of Costa Rica. This is where God's perfect plan for my life begins. As a result of the above meetings, a Christian political party offered me the opportunity to represent their party as a candidate for congressional office. I had no intention of venturing into politics, or being a congressman no less, so I rejected the offer. My focus had always been ministry.

However, there was a restlessness in my heart, and I decided to pray to the Lord about this opportunity. In response to my prayer, God told me, "You have to enter through the doors that I am going to open for you." The idea still seemed impossible. Historically, very few Christian congressmen had been elected. I continued to pray during the following weeks, and to my surprise, other political parties also came to offer me a candidacy as a congressman. Days later, I attended a meeting of pastors in Mexico City. While we were praying, a pastor approached me and gave me a word. Without knowing anything about what was happening to me, he told me exactly which proposal I should accept. As soon as I returned to Costa Rica, I obeyed the voice of God.

With only ten days left until the registration deadline, I accepted the offer of the second party that had visited me, which was also a Christian political party. Humanly, it would have been impossible for me to have been elected, because in addition to our party occupying third place in the province of San Jose, never had a Christian political party obtained more than one congressional position in the capital. However, the Holy Spirit brought a season of supernatural grace, and our party's candidate for president of Costa Rica managed, in one week, to ascend from eighth place to fourth place in public opinion polls, and the following week, he was in second place. Miraculously, in the national elections, for the first time in the history of our country, our party gained fourteen Christian congressmen nationwide.

Currently, 25 percent of the congressmen are Christians. We are very much strengthened in the Lord, and we trust that our hard work in this parliament will result in Costa Rica having its first Christian president in the election of 2020. With this governmental platform, we plan to strengthen the Christian principles and values that our nation has been losing. In addition, this opening in government has brought an opportunity to introduce Jesus to other congressmen. We met

THERE IS NO PURPOSE WITHOUT A SEASON,
AND NO SEASON WITHOUT A PURPOSE.

with the president of the republic on several occasions, taking the opportunity to pray for him and bless him.

The most important thing is that my work in government has not affected my work as a pastor, which is still my priority. In the last four years, our church has applied many of the spiritual principles that Apostle Maldonado implements in his ministry. One of these is the "21-Day Breakthrough Fast," which has unleashed many miracles of healing, as well as the restoration of marriages, cancellation of debts, financing for the purchase of houses and vehicles, and provision of jobs. The model of intercession developed by Prophet Ana Maldonado has become a powerful weapon of battle for us that has propelled our ministry, bringing revelation of the Word and causing our church to grow. Today, I can affirm that the supernatural power of God has manifested in an accelerated and explosive way over our life, and His grace has allowed me to experience His "good, pleasing, and perfect will." (See Romans 12:2.)

WHAT IS DONE OUT OF NEED WILL ONLY HAVE A TEMPORARY EFFECT, BUT WHAT IS DONE ACCORDING TO GOD'S PURPOSE WILL HAVE ETERNAL SIGNIFICANCE.

FROM A CHILDHOOD OF LACK TO THE MAJOR LEAGUES

Carlos Zambrano's career as a pitcher in Major League Baseball is known to people throughout the world. Through different seasons in his life, the Lord has taken him to his true purpose as a leader in the kingdom of God, to "pitch" the gospel to the sports world. The following is his testimony:

> As a child, growing up in a small town in Venezuela, I had two big dreams—playing Major League Baseball in the United States and being used by God as a preacher, ministering to crowds. My life was not very easy, and I knew that the possibility of my reaching the big leagues was remote. During that time, I would often search for God. I was raised in a Christian home and attended church, and I always knew that God had a purpose for my life. So, at age thirteen, I decided to follow one of my dreams, and I joined a baseball team. At first, I was not very good, but I had a passion for the sport. One day, in the middle of a game, I was chosen to be the pitcher. I remember throwing the ball as far as I could, with all my strength, and we beat the other team with that pitch. When the game was over, a man who had been a spectator approached me and gave me some advice that helped me delineate my career. He told me that I had a gift as a pitcher and that I should change to that position in the

field. After that, I began to work more and more on my physical conditioning as a pitcher.

Although I had a natural talent for baseball, there have been times in my life when God has used others to help me see what He sees in me: His purpose. In my life, each new season has been marked by people who have given me the right word. I eventually became a famous baseball pitcher, playing in the major leagues for the Chicago Cubs and the Miami Marlins. Unfortunately, while pursuing my dream of being a professional baseball player, I had forgotten my other dream, which was to be used by God to preach His Word. Although my wife went to church, I strayed from God's way and lost my fellowship with Him. I started going out to clubs and drinking alcohol, and I walked away completely. However, even though I was sunken in sin, God did not stop showing me His unconditional love.

One day, when I was in Guatemala, I suddenly felt dizzy, my heart began to beat irregularly, and my blood pressure rose and fell. I seemed to be on the verge of death. The doctors from the Chicago club immediately saw me. They ran all kinds of tests, but they did not find anything wrong with my physical health. Even so, I continued to feel sick, and I felt as if I was under enormous stress. Back in Venezuela, I went to see my personal doctor, a Christian professional who knows both the medical and spiritual aspects of life, and I was able to understand what was happening to me. He told me, "Carlos, we have done all the tests and there is nothing physically wrong. What is happening to you is spiritual, my friend. God is calling you, and He is giving you a chance."

Those words initiated a transformation in me, leading me to seek God and learn about His kingdom. When I accepted Christ into my heart and let Him live in me, it was the biggest decision

SCARCITY FOSTERS NEED, AND NEED GENERATES POVERTY.

I had ever made. Before that, I had been focused on material matters and vanities, but I didn't have any peace. I was always angry and stressed. Receiving Christ and His love was the best thing that could have happened to me—better than winning the Cy Young Award (an annual prize for the best pitchers in Major League Baseball) or the world championship of baseball. Nothing compares to the love of God in my heart.

Today, my family is happy, and I have peace in my heart, knowing that God directs my life. I've never again felt like I was about to die, because I have an intimate and permanent relationship with God. But I also have had to admit that I cannot handle everything on my own. I prayed to God for a mentor, someone who could be a model for me in Christ and correct me. Then, I was invited to a Supernatural Encounter meeting in Caracas, Venezuela, in which Apostle Maldonado was preaching. When the music group began to play, I felt my legs weakening in that heavenly atmosphere. The apostle gave me a word from God about something no one else knew, and from that point on, he became my spiritual father and mentor. He taught me that there is a thin line between a career and a call, and I believe that, after all my achievements on the baseball field, God has called me to be a leader in His kingdom, to minister what He has imparted to my life.

Now, my second dream is being fulfilled. I am a pastor sent by Apostle Maldonado to my home country of Venezuela, and we have established a church there. I also exercise my pastoral call by telling other professional baseball players what God has taught me in this season of my life, ministering to their hearts with the love of God, praying for their families, and leaving a legacy on this earth for the glory of God.

My best friend, who grew up with me, is my disciple today, and he is in charge of a House of Peace connected with our church in Venezuela that has more than three hundred people. When I am not in Venezuela, he directs everything for the church.

My friend also has a testimony about the supernatural power of God. The day after Apostle Maldonado had ministered to me at the Supernatural Encounter in Caracas, my friend and his wife agreed to go with me to attend another meeting. At the time, they were separated. My friend was living with his parents and his wife was living with her mother, and they were in the process of getting a divorce. They didn't want anything to do with each other. However, during this meeting, Apostle Maldonado called them forward and ministered to them. He did not know that they were about to get a divorce, but he gave them a word from God, saying that the Lord was going to restore their marriage. Today, my friend's family is completely restored. He and his wife have a beautiful marriage and are serving God.

LIVING FOR A PURPOSE

A PERSON IN CONSTANT NEED OFTEN REMAINS IMMATURE,
BECAUSE THEIR NEED MAKES THEM SELFISH.

6

LIVING FOR A PURPOSE

Most people tend to make decisions in life based on their immediate and temporary needs, not according to their God-given purpose. This leads many of them to have an existence characterized by lack, because they spend most of their time focusing on what to eat, what to wear, where to live, how to provide for their family, how to pay for their children's education, and so on. This mind-set has been taken advantage of by marketing strategists, who not only specialize in playing up these needs, but also in creating a range of new, perceived needs for people to dwell on.

A number of people, including Christians, live in a bubble of consumerism, where the most important goal is to be able to afford whatever they want. If they don't have the money, that's what their credit cards are for! This is why we see people working hard in order to obtain "the car of the year," the latest phone or computer, vacations in the most exclusive places, designer clothes, the house of their dreams, and anything else that projects a status of wealth. This is one reason for the abundance of personal debt we see in the world today. It is also a contributor to poverty.

GOD MEETS US IN THE PLACE OF OUR NEED,
BUT HE SUPPLIES US AT THE POINT OF OUR FAITH.

Sadly, the church as a whole isn't making much of a difference in changing people's attitudes about lack and consumerism. Some pastors preach messages that serve these same skewed priorities, rather than promoting a renewal of people's minds by teaching them how to fulfill their purpose. If people continually hear messages from the pulpit about their need or how they should reach for material blessings, they will begin to unite with their scarcity and feed off of it, all the while becoming even needier. Then, if they do happen to hear a message about purpose, they feel that this message doesn't apply to them, but only to others.

Those who constantly struggle with their finances are not able to grow or prosper. Neither do they have any extra funds or other resources to give to the work of God. They become trapped by a vicious cycle of focusing on and satisfying their needs, and therefore have no time to pursue and fulfill their purpose. Without a doubt, this is a strategy of the devil!

For that reason, whenever I gather pastors and other leaders who are under my spiritual covering, I urge them to change their way of preaching. I ask them to stop focusing on needs, because the people are already well aware of them. Instead, I urge them to begin teaching about the principles that govern God's purpose, so that the people's thinking will be transformed and their needs can be met.

I do not want you to misunderstand me. In everyday life, many of our needs have an economic framework, but there are, of course, other vital concerns. I do not mean that we should ignore the needs of those who suffer from financial difficulty or any other problem, such as illness or depression. Jesus commands us to have compassion on those who are needy—to pray for them and help them. Many people come to King Jesus Ministry with physical, financial, emotional, mental, or spiritual needs. We take care of everything properly! We give food to the hungry, visit the sick, minister to the imprisoned, and do social work. However, without a doubt, the greatest need people have is an emptiness in their soul that can only be filled by God. Therefore, we should not stop at meeting people's immediate needs; we should empower them know God and to prosper in all areas of their life. We must teach them about their purpose and guide them out of the cycle of need and into God's plans for them.

AT THE MERCY OF NEED

Until a person enters into their purpose, they will always be at the mercy of their needs. Sadly, many religious and secular organizations are still motivated solely by a desire to address people's lack. They have not had the revelation that the kingdom of God advances by fulfilling purpose, not by supplying needs. Their approach actually serves to restrict divine provision, because then people's capacity to receive remains small; it is limited to their immediate needs, so they are unable to obtain the abundance God desires to give them. Neither can people commit to a vision because they are too busy attending to their everyday necessities.

The person who lives according to their need often becomes self-focused and even selfish. Need becomes their idol because they seek first to satisfy their own lack, while neglecting the matters of the kingdom. The Bible tells us, "*Therefore do not worry, saying, 'What shall we eat?' or 'What shall we drink?' or 'What shall we wear?'... But seek first the kingdom of God and His righteousness, and all these things shall be added to you*" (Matthew 6:31, 33).

THOSE WHO LIVE IN NEED WILL LACK ACCESS TO PROVISION, BECAUSE THIS ACCESS IS CONNECTED TO PURPOSE.

Need often leads us to seek God. However, God usually does not move out of need alone; instead, He moves where there is faith. (See, for example, Hebrews 11:6.) God has infinite abundance, while human beings have great needs due to our fallen nature and the fallen world in which we live. The meeting point between God's abundance and man's need is a place in eternity called the "altar." In this place, we can be freed of depression, disease, hatred, jealousy, a desire for revenge, suicidal thoughts, vices of all kinds, scarcity, debt, poverty, fear, persecution, disbelief, inner emptiness, loneliness, anguish, and much more. At this altar, God supplies all human needs—not so we will remain at that point, but so we can be free to fulfill our purpose.

We all have needs of various kinds. This will be the case as long as we live on earth. But we must receive the revelation that God will *supply* all our needs. Once these needs have been met, we cannot stay in a need-based mentality. We must learn to live for a purpose. The Bible emphatically affirms, *"And my God shall supply all your need according to His riches in glory by Christ Jesus"* (Philippians 4:19). Life really begins for us when we start to fulfill God's purpose. Never sacrifice your purpose for your need.

Many people go to church seeking to have their immediate needs met, whether spiritual, financial, physical, or emotional. Sadly, when their needs are addressed, a number of them do not continue to attend church. They feel that they have done the hard work of getting what they required, so they have no more reason to go there. Thus, when some people receive a blessing, they say, "Wonderful! I no longer have to keep fighting in the Spirit!" When they receive healing, they declare, "I can now stop fasting and seeking God!" When they finally establish a business or close a lucrative sales deal, they think, "I am really talented! I no longer have to look for God's help!" After their marriage is restored, their children return home, or their family conflicts calm down, they pronounce, "Our problems are over! Why keep praying to God?" Some people even say, in effect, "God should just leave me alone now and attend to others who need help more than I do."

Such people don't understand how essential it is to develop a close relationship with God and to support, and receive support from, other Christians. But those who understand God's priorities recognize that as they continue to attend worship services, receive training in discipleship, enter into a mentor relationship with a mature believer, and learn to love God with all their heart, soul, and mind, God will strengthen them to fulfill their purpose.

If you never receive a revelation of your purpose, you will continue to think that you should seek God only when you have a need you can't meet on your own. But that is a lifestyle in which you merely "serve time" and never live in the joy of the Lord and the seasons of abundance God has prepared for you.

FOUR STAGES IN LIVING FOR A PURPOSE

As we come to understand and live in our purpose, we often pass through the following four stages, through which God leads us to fulfill the plans He has for us.

NEED-BASED LIVING

As I expressed above, every person on earth will always be subject to spiritual, emotional, mental, physical, material, relational, or other needs. We know that needs are a part of our daily lives. But why do we have needs? Before the fall, human beings lived a supernatural lifestyle. In Eden, all their needs were met. Yet Adam and Eve disobeyed God, breaking their communion with Him and His Spirit. When the human race fell, then sickness, poverty, hunger, and slavery became commonplace.

Is God unable to supply the needs of His creation? Beloved reader, God has more than enough to supply all our needs. However, our sin separates us from Him. The second Adam—Jesus Christ, the Son of God—came to earth to restore our communion with the Father. Through His death and resurrection, Jesus enables us to be forgiven and remain close to God, so that all our needs may be met. *"For without Me you can do nothing"* (John 15:5). Now, we can confidently come before the throne of God's grace, *"that we may obtain mercy and find grace to help in time of need"* (Hebrews 4:16). As a Father, God wants to supply what we lack. He does not want us to live according to need, but according to purpose. However, most people stay in the stage of need all of their lives, and never move on.

RECEIVING MIRACLES

In God's infinite mercy, He sent Jesus to restore us to the realm of the supernatural. However, if we

GOD HAS MORE THAN ENOUGH TO SUPPLY ALL OUR NEEDS.

do not enter into our purpose, we will still experience the effects of living in a "fallen-man" state. When the apostle Paul entered into his purpose, his life took a 180-degree turn. Although he went through various seasons, they were all marked by two elements: the preaching of the gospel of the kingdom, and the manifestation of the power of God through miracles. (See, for example, Acts 19:11.)

We all need a miracle in our life of some sort, and God wants us to move from lack into His miraculous provision. We don't receive a miracle by following mere religion, because religion cannot provide the faith or power to bring it about. Only God can produce a miracle, and He wants to do a miracle in your life now. Miracles still happen! Believe for one! What's more, I challenge you to include the word *miracle* in your everyday vocabulary. The Scriptures say that *"Jesus Christ is the same yesterday, today, and forever"* (Hebrews 13:8). This means that since Jesus did miracles in the past, He will do them today, and He will continue to do them forever. We must understand that God does not want us to merely receive isolated miracles in our lives. He wants us to live in the power of the supernatural in a continuous way. But this can happen only when we enter into our purpose.

DISCOVERING PURPOSE

God knows us according to our purpose, not according to our need. The person who lives in need will always be at the mercy of the enemy's temptations and attacks. But the person who lives in alignment with their purpose can resist the devil (see James 4:7), because they know who they are, and God supports them because they do His will.

Those who live according to God's plans do not waste time making decisions based on need. Instead, all their decisions are based on their purpose. They do not conform to the erroneous or negative words other people say about them; rather, they live by what God says about them. No one is able to sabotage them, no matter how hard they try.

The individual who walks in their purpose is more powerful than their opposition; thus, such a person cannot be prevented from growing and doing God's will.

LIVING IN POWER

When we live according to need, we are always looking for quick remedies. If we suffer a crisis, all alarms are triggered, and the problem captures our full attention. We then look for someone who can get us out of our dilemma. As we have seen, most churches only try to "calm" the needs of the people because they lack supernatural power to offer definitive solutions. That's why most people remain in a state of lack, unable to find an adequate answer to their needs. They are stopped from moving to the next stage, where they could receive miracles by faith, and from the subsequent stages, where they could begin to live out their purpose and be filled with God's power.

The power of God is the answer to all your problems because it is unlimited and eternal. It goes above and beyond reason, education, science, and natural laws. Without the power of God, we cannot fulfill our purpose, meet the needs of others, leave a legacy, or transform generations. Only the power of God can overcome the impossible circumstances human beings face.

Thus, the maximum stage in which a human being can live is the stage in which they experience the continuous power of God in their life. This level is

TO WALK IN OUR PURPOSE IS TO SEE OURSELVES AS GOD SEES US.

found in the realm of the supernatural, where we can live as God designed us to. It is where the fulfillment of our purpose crystallizes.

We must make the transition from a mentality of need to an outlook of purpose. Whoever takes the path of purpose will leave mediocrity behind and move toward excellence; they will go from poverty to prosperity and from lack to abundance. They will live in the eternal realm as they progress in God's plans for their life. When we walk in our purpose, we live in surplus—excess, superabundance—because we have access to the provision that God has assigned to our calling on earth. When you merely desire to meet your needs, you essentially discard your surplus and live in shortage. In fact, as soon as you meet one need, another will soon appear, because you only know how to live from need to need.

THE KINGDOM VERSUS NEED

The kingdom of God never stops advancing, growing, and developing; it is always in expansion mode because that is God's priority. Any monetary surplus that He gives us will always be for the purpose of financing the extension of His kingdom, the preaching of the gospel, and the "increase of His peace" (see Isaiah 9:7), until every person has heard of Christ and His kingdom. God will not prosper us just to meet our needs. He will prosper us when we begin to expand His kingdom and preach His gospel. This means that our purpose will always be intimately related to the advancement of the kingdom. When we understand that revelation, we will never experience shortage again. Unfortunately, for many people, their needs are more important to them than the kingdom of God. That is why they remain in a cycle of scarcity, living every day just to supply their needs.

On the cross, Jesus paid for all our needs. This means that more than two thousand years ago, God's provision was made available for us!

If fact, before the foundation of the world, the Father gave us purpose and provided for us. (See Ephesians 1:4–5.) There is a purpose and territory assigned specifically to you that does not compete with anyone else's. Are you governing your territory according to the purpose that God gave you? Is your first priority pleasing God and advancing His kingdom? When you are aligned with God's plans, your purpose will always be greater than your need. When you fulfill your purpose, El Shaddai, God Almighty, fights on your behalf!

Therefore, if we obey God and focus on the advancement of His kingdom, all of our needs will be met. When we put God first—including His kingdom, His gospel, and our relationship with Him—we will see excess and abundance in all areas of our life.

WHAT WILL YOU BE KNOWN FOR?

What will you be known for on the earth—being a person of purpose or a person of need? It would be tragic if the only record we left on earth was one of need. Are you someone who always must be given to, or someone who has something to give? Are you someone who always has a shortage, or someone who is able to produce excess in order to supply what others lack?

I pray that you will break away from a mentality of need and make the transition to the viewpoint of the kingdom, motivated by a desire to expand God's

GOD'S PLAN IS TO BRING US TO KNOW OUR PURPOSE AND TO MEET ALL OUR NEEDS WITH HIS SUPERNATURAL POWER.

reign and serve others. To advance the kingdom is to bring heaven to earth. It is to manifest the supernatural power of God to every person and in every situation. It is to lead people to salvation and the fulfillment of God's purposes for them, so that Christ may be glorified. It is to bring the life of heaven to the world—impacting individuals, families, cities, and nations with God's peace, love, and provision.

This is a time of increase! When we are in our purpose, the anointing of the increase is always working in us. Today, God wants us to live in His eternal life—a satisfying life, full of joy, peace, love, and a sense of belonging and destiny. We do not have to wait until we die to have eternal life; we can enjoy it here and now!

If you have received this revelation about living according to the purpose for which you were created, I want to pray for you now:

> Father God, I pray that You will supply every need that my readers have. I declare that if their bodies are sick, they are healed now. I declare that if they are depressed, discouraged, or distressed, they are free now. I declare that if they need a miracle in body, soul, or spirit, they receive it now. For those who lack an organ or another part of their body, I declare that it is created now—there are new livers, new kidneys, new skin, and even new bones. For those who need a miracle in their family, I proclaim that they receive it now. For those who need a financial miracle, I pronounce that it is done now. For those who are hurt and offended, having pain in their souls, I declare that they are healthy now. I bind and cast out the spirits of hatred, anger, resentment, and guilt, and I release the love of God upon them, now! I destroy the mentality of mediocrity. I break every scheme of the enemy against them and anything else that is hindering them. I declare that they all walk in their purpose, now! In the name of Jesus, amen.

At this time, all needs are being met, so make the decision to live for your purpose. I am empowered to be successful in my family, ministry, and business because I live for the purpose that God gave me. Today, I release that same way of life over you. Be empowered to thrive in every area of your life. Seek the kingdom of God first. Seek God in everything you do, and all that you need will be provided. Look for the revelation of your purpose so that your life can be full and happy. There is a higher level of living than just existing to secure shelter, clothing, and food for yourself and your family. Live for your purpose, expand the kingdom, and let God supply all that you need.

WHEN A PERSON FINDS THEIR PURPOSE, THEY ALSO FIND THEIR PROSPERITY.

TESTIMONIES OF FINDING AND FULFILLING PURPOSE

A LIFE OF PURPOSE IN FINANCIAL CONSULTING

Janelle connected with King Jesus Ministry during an event we sponsored in Malaysia. The supernatural power of God awoke within her the purpose for her life, and today she is a successful businesswoman. This is her testimony:

> I went with a group of friends to an event in Kuala Lumpur, Malaysia, conducted by Apostle Guillermo Maldonado. We thought it was rather transcendent to have a Christian crusade in a Muslim stadium, so we had to attend. We really believed that our gifts were in the realm of serving others, so we had the expectation of being activated in them. At that conference, we witnessed the power of God and saw how an atmosphere for miracles is created. And miracles happened! The testimonies impressed us greatly. One man had been mute for thirty-three years. He had been born deaf in his right ear and had only 15 percent hearing in his left ear. His only ways of communicating were through sign language and certain devices. During the encounter, after this man received the command to have faith, God created new eardrums in him, and that very day, he was able to emit his first vocal sounds. But that was not all!
>
> A woman testified that she had suffered a stroke, leaving her with serious aftereffects. She could not walk and had severe kidney failure. But during the time of prayer, Apostle Maldonado sent a word of healing, and she was able to get out of her wheelchair and stand up by herself. It was glorious! In addition, we witnessed the movement of the Holy Spirit. The impact on us was such that we wanted to go beyond that single experience. We traveled to the United States to receive training at the University

of the Supernatural Ministry at King Jesus Ministry in Miami. There, the apostle spoke to us about "mega-faith" and how God wanted to give us mega-projects and blessings, and to unleash our purpose.

I felt as though I had been waiting for this all my life. I received a word that an expansion was coming, but I did not know exactly what to expect, so I began to stretch my faith. Suddenly, I felt the call of God to be in the field of financial business planning. Days later in Singapore, God provided me with financial increase—I gained in two days what usually would have taken three months. That was the beginning. Now, my purpose is to finance and develop business through the supernatural power of God. I have learned to stop seeing with my natural eyes and see with spiritual eyes instead. My financial consulting company is now expanding. We have put God first, and we dedicate time to prayer, to being alone with the Father. He is leading us to fulfill our purpose and to be a blessing to many others with our testimony.

OUR PRIORITIES DETERMINE THE FLOW OF OUR LIFE—IF THEY ARE NOT ALIGNED WITH GOD, THERE WILL BE DISORDER, CHAOS, CONFUSION, AND LACK.

FROM UNIVERSITY STUDENTS TO INFLUENTIAL BLOGGERS

My name is Esperanza, and my husband, Sebastián, and I have become successful social media bloggers from the United States. When I met Sebastian, I could see that he was the person God had chosen for me. We complement one another and grow in our purpose together through what we create.

In school, I studied to be a journalist, with a dream of becoming a TV news anchor, and my husband studied to be an architect. Our project on social media began the first month of our marriage. We were ready for our future, but very few doors opened. And then, God moved. Today, I can say that we have seen His glory over our lives, including financial provision, since the first appearance of our lifestyle blog on social networks.

The blog started as something fun, but soon the number of our followers grew, which brought an economic benefit to our lives. Today, we have close to half a million followers. Our success has been so great that our income allows us to work in social media full-time. Our blog has served as a platform to achieve our purpose.

At the beginning, it was difficult not having a fixed salary. Some months would be very slow, while other months would be financially explosive. In such an environment, strong character is required to stand firm in one's principles, because when big commercial brands see that you have a large number of followers, they want to collaborate with you. Due to our success in social media, we have been offered jobs with various companies that are recognized worldwide, but we have rejected certain proposals because we do not agree with the ethics of the products or the merchants. We conduct ourselves in a distinct way from many people in this environment. Saying no to a number of projects that have been presented to us is what has differentiated us in the market. From the beginning, we made clear what lines we would not cross. Big advertisers and other bloggers have noticed the difference. We have been able to help others understand that social networks can be a platform to express one's ideas without compromising one's principles.

We have seen God glorify Himself, not only in our purpose, but also in our personal life. We have always put Him first, and this has helped us to be positioned in a place of privilege and influence. God eventually opened doors for us with a brand, and this has given us the opportunity to travel the world. Basically, we and the brand have benefited one another. As "influential" people in social media, we have seen the impact of our opinions and way of life. Today, much of our time is spent with bloggers and others who work in social media. We have even been able to spiritually help some of them and make a difference in their lives with our testimony. With our platforms on social networks, we have been able to reach not only Christians, but all kinds of people, including Buddhists and atheists.

I am grateful to God because in every detail of my life, I see His powerful right hand. I owe everything to Him. Without God, we

WHEN WE ARE LIVING IN OUR PURPOSE, WE CAN MEET THE NEEDS OF OTHERS, BECAUSE WE WILL HAVE A SURPLUS.

could not have done it! My husband and I know that this is just the beginning of what He is doing through our lives, and we are so grateful for what is to come. Knowing and fulfilling our purpose in God as a married couple is the most precious thing that could have happened to us. We thank Him because, in our position, we can fulfill His purpose for our life.

THE POWER OF PURPOSE

A PERSON IN NEED CANNOT HELP OTHERS. OUR SEED MULTIPLIES WHEN WE SOW ACCORDING TO A PURPOSE, NOT A NEED.

7

THE POWER OF PURPOSE

Being aligned with God's original intention for us brings joy, peace, and power. Nothing can compare to this! When we follow our purpose, it gives us a full life, with the satisfaction of knowing we are pleasing God. I often say, "I never tire of thanking God because I get paid to do what I love. I am rewarded for fulfilling His purpose for my life. There is no money, fame, prestige, or position that can buy that blessing!"

The supernatural power of God is indispensable for achieving our calling. However, there are those who think that God's power is solely for bringing people to salvation and producing miracles, healings, and deliverances. They don't see how it is necessary to fulfill all aspects of their purpose. Therefore, in this chapter, I want to share with you the wisdom of the Holy Spirit about this very important topic. The following are some of the many ways in which purpose energizes our calling, while overcoming all hindrances to achieving our destiny.

THE ACTIVATING POWER OF PURPOSE

THE POWER TO GUIDE US TO OUR DESTINY

Let me reaffirm the fact that without a purpose, no one can travel their true path on this earth. They will not be able to go anywhere in life or make an impact on the world. Purpose has the power to lead us to our destiny because it gives us meaning and direction. It reveals our path and orders our steps. We gain a sense of where we are going, so we can do what it takes to arrive there.

When we follow what God has destined for us to do, our efforts will be successful. For example, an important part of Jesus's purpose was to heal people. (See Luke 4:18–19.) Therefore, because He remained in communion with His Father and continually followed His will, it was enough for Him to tell a leper, *"I am willing; be cleansed"* (Matthew 8:3), and the leper was healed. In addition, Jesus was destined to rise from the dead, and that is why He did not remain in the grave but was resurrected by the Spirit of God. (See, for example, Acts 2:22–24.) Similarly, the power of your purpose will lead you to achieve your destiny.

THE ROAD TO YOUR DESTINY BEGINS WITH THE KNOWLEDGE OF YOUR PURPOSE. ONLY THOSE WHO KNOW WHERE THEY ARE GOING ARE WILLING TO PAY THE COST OF GETTING THERE.

THE POWER OF INFLUENCE

Purpose also has the power of influence. Your sphere of influence relates to the "territory" God has given you to carry out your calling. That territory might be a family, community, vocation, region, or some other area in which your presence, knowledge, and abilities give you influence. Our influence often extends over several areas.

When you know your purpose, you can "mark" your territory and establish your sphere of influence. You can't exert your God-given influence unless you are in the proper territory. There are people who want to fulfill their purpose in the wrong territory, and this only frustrates them because they don't yield any fruit. Since purpose determines our sphere of influence, then the place where we will be the most influential is where our purpose lies.

THE POWER TO BE UNIQUE

Those who find their purpose cease to have anything in common with what is commonplace. They think and act differently from others. Unlike many people today, they do not seek entertainment. Instead, they look for what will lead them to advance in carrying out the purpose that burns within them. While others seek temporary satisfaction, people of purpose seek what is eternal. While others settle for meeting their basic needs, people of purpose work to leave an abundant inheritance to subsequent generations. While others accumulate money and material goods for themselves, people of purpose sow into people's lives and work to raise up those within their sphere of influence.

THE POWER TO PRODUCE CHANGE

Purpose confronts the status quo, the obsolete, and the routine. It challenges mediocrity, stale religion, empty tradition, and mindless conformity. Purpose defies *"old wineskins"* (see Matthew 9:16–17); it

KNOWING THAT YOU HAVE BEEN DESTINED TO FULFILL GOD'S PURPOSE SETS YOUR WAY OF THINKING, YOUR HABITS, AND YOUR DISCIPLINE.

challenges established policies and ways of doing things that are no longer beneficial—or were never helpful in the first place.

If you do not change, you are not living in your purpose, because God's purpose always produces positive change. Are you challenging an outdated status quo with the purpose God has given you? Are you doing something to change the world for the better?

THE POWER OF CREATIVITY

A person who isn't functioning in their purpose lacks the power to create and expand. They may make a living, but they will not be able to generate a surplus. Only purpose gives us the power to prosper beyond meeting our basic needs. It provides us with an excess that allows us to produce something new, take risks, go beyond what other people are doing, and achieve what others only dare to dream.

In our ministry, I often see people creating from their purpose. We have hundreds of testimonies from individuals who, with a creative idea from God, have achieved a promotion at work, are enjoying business success, or are receiving profits from an invention. Certain individuals—some who were employed when they started attending King Jesus Ministry, others who had no job—are now prosperous entrepreneurs, people of purpose whom God has anointed and to whom He has given power, grace, and favor. All of these people are helping to advance the kingdom of God on earth due to a creative idea that came as a result of knowing their purpose. It is time to awaken the creative power of your purpose so that you can develop innovative ideas, businesses, inventions, products, systems, protocols, books, songs, or anything else God has called you to do.

THE POWER TO PROSPER

"And you shall remember the LORD your God, for it is He who gives you power to get wealth…" (Deuteronomy 8:18). The person whose thoughts are aligned with their purpose has the power to create wealth because their thoughts come from God. Thus, when someone discovers their purpose, they find their prosperity. As we have seen, God always provides for the fulfillment of His *entire* purpose for our life, not just for our temporary needs. His provision comes in the form of resources, connections, favor, time, and relationships. It would not make sense for the Creator of the universe to assign someone a task or give them a purpose, and then not provide them with the power or resources to accomplish it. He is a God of abundance!

On earth, there are five types of wealth: that which is earned, inherited, borrowed, stolen, or created. Anything that is created always begins with an idea. For example, in the field of finances, Warren Buffett found his purpose in business. At age eleven, while other children played, he began to invest in the stock market in a small way with money from his own earnings. He continued to earn money and make business investments. Then, after obtaining degrees in business and forming lucrative partnerships, Buffett acquired a textile manufacturing company and, from it, began to create other companies, diversify products, and multiply profits, until he built a corporate empire that includes insurance, railroads, appliances, newspapers, airlines, soft drinks, food, furniture, clothing, and utility companies. Today, he is one of the richest men in the world, and he has given away a high percentage of his fortune.

WHEN WE FIND OUR PURPOSE, WE STOP BEING "ONE OF THE BUNCH" AND BECOME DISTINCT.

God wants to release abundance and even over-abundance in every area of your life through your purpose. Your short-term needs usually demand urgent attention, but they will not last. Your purpose as a human being is aligned with the purposes of the kingdom of God, and therefore it is eternal. A divine purpose is required to give birth to an earthly purpose, upon which God will pour out His surplus. As a Father, God will supply all your essential needs (see, for example, Matthew 6:26), but if you want to live in plenty, you will have to discover your purpose—and your power—in Him.

THE POWER TO MAKE US "KNOWN" IN HEAVEN

"And I saw the dead, small and great, standing before God, and books were opened. And another book was opened, which is the Book of Life. And the dead were judged according to their works, by the things which were written in the books" (Revelation 20:12). Although God knows everything about us, purpose makes us "known" to Him in the sense that heaven is making a record of our works, not for the sake of determining our eternal destiny—salvation is attained only through grace and faith—but rather for granting rewards to those who have been good stewards of what God has given them to fulfill their purpose on earth. Heaven is now recording the purposes and works of our generation. For example, I am known for ministering God's supernatural power, and in heaven there is a book being written about my purpose and what I am doing to fulfill it. A similar book is being written about your life.

THE OVERCOMING POWER OF PURPOSE

As we move toward our calling, there are many ways in which our true purpose can be challenged, not only by outside forces, but also by ourselves. Yet if we continue to keep our eyes on God and His destiny for our lives, the power of our purpose will enable us to meet every one of those challenges.

MORE POWERFUL THAN ANY PLAN

We can make various plans for ourselves, and each one of them may be very good, but God has something even more powerful than our plans: His purpose. You might spend your entire life planning but still never reach your potential or achieve the fullness of God's will that will enable you to leave a legacy on earth. It is better to discover and devote yourself to the perfect plan designed specifically for you by the Father.

Remember that before we drew up any of our own plans, our Father had already established a divine purpose for our life. His purpose for us precedes our plans, and it is designed to fit us exactly. When we follow our own plans, without having a purpose to guide us, we find ourselves constantly making detours. However, when we follow our God-given purpose, everything flows in a forward direction, even though we will have to overcome obstacles and the attacks of the enemy. God's timing and parameters for our calling are perfect.

We have seen that when people lack purpose, their time on earth can be frustrating and meaningless. They become discontented with their daily lives because they follow plans that have nothing to do with their calling. They work ceaselessly, struggle, and become fatigued over endeavors that were never assigned to them, and for which they were not designed. There is no satisfaction in that.

SOMEONE WHO LIVES ACCORDING TO THEIR PURPOSE WILL ALWAYS BE AN AGENT OF CHANGE IN SOCIETY.

Have you ever eaten a meal and been full, but not satisfied? Usually, it is because something seems lacking in the food's variety or taste. That is how it is with many people who lack purpose. Their lives may be filled with many undertakings, but they do not find satisfaction in them because they are involved in activities they were not created for, which makes them feel incomplete. They can never experience total fulfillment, regardless of how many plans they make, because those plans are limited and temporary. God's purpose is the key to living a life of true and lasting meaning. "*There are many plans in a man's heart, nevertheless the Lord's counsel—that will stand*" (Proverbs 19:21).

God knows that nothing will make us happier and more complete than His original intention for us, because His purpose and our existence are intimately linked. Therefore, if you want to please God and live well, you *must* discover and follow God's purpose for your life.

MORE POWERFUL THAN ANY PROBLEM

There is no situation, however adverse, that can stop God's purpose for our lives. To better understand this truth, let's look at the life of the apostle Paul, who reported undergoing hardships for the sake of the gospel, "*in weariness and toil, in sleeplessness often, in hunger and thirst, in fastings often, in cold and nakedness*" (2 Corinthians 11:27). Despite all that Paul went through, he remained firm in his purpose. This tells us that when we experience problems, it does not necessarily mean that we are displeasing God or that we are separated from His will. Jesus told us, *"In the world you will have tribulation; but be of good cheer, I have overcome the world"* (John 16:33).

MORE POWERFUL THAN ANY DISAPPOINTMENT

Along the path to fulfilling our destiny, we will go through various disappointments. Jesus experienced disappointments, too, and so did His apostles. I have also experienced them, and I am sure that many other leaders in the church have as well. The most dangerous aspect of disappointments is that they bring a strong temptation to give up. But if we know our purpose and maintain an intimate relationship with the Father, we will not give up. The purpose that burns within us is more powerful than our disappointment.

In the Old Testament, we read about the prophet Jeremiah, who proclaimed God's warnings to His people about their sin, and the dire consequences of their continued disobedience. Those messages brought Jeremiah opposition, persecution, and the threat of death. He must have suffered many disappointments and discouragements because he admitted the following:

> *The word of the LORD was made to me a reproach and a derision daily. Then I said, "I will not make mention of Him, nor speak anymore in His name." But His word was in my heart like a burning fire shut up in my bones; I was weary of holding it back, and I could not.* (Jeremiah 20:8–9)

Jeremiah was tempted to give up, but his purpose, which was like a burning fire within him, prevailed.

THE PERSON WHO THINKS IN TERMS OF THEIR PURPOSE WILL CREATE FROM THOSE THOUGHTS.

MORE POWERFUL THAN ANY OPPOSITION

The power of God working in our lives to accomplish our purpose is greater than any opposition we may face, whether it is from the enemy, our own fears, or the persecution of others. As believers in Jesus Christ, we have been given the ability to defeat Satan's plans. *"For this purpose the Son of God was manifested, that He might destroy the works of the devil"* (1 John 3:8). This means that in the power of God's Spirit, we can rise above our weaknesses, overcome the enemy on the battlefield of life, and recapture everything he has stolen from us. Moses faced Pharaoh, David faced Goliath, and Jesus faced sin and death, but in each case, the power of God was there to give them the victory.

What adversary are you facing? For many people, their chief adversary is fear. They know what they have to do, but the fear of failure paralyzes them. Some people fear the opinions, criticism, or rejection of others. If you remain in your purpose, God will give you the power to defeat these fears—no matter how gigantic they may seem—and fulfill the purpose He has given you.

I stated earlier that no one can sabotage a person who lives by their purpose. However, we must be prepared to be persecuted as we move toward fulfilling our destiny. In fact, persecution is one of the clearest signs that you are walking in your calling. The enemy does not harass a person who has mere plans; rather, he persecutes people who have a specific purpose because they are able to overturn his evil schemes.

Jesus was heavily persecuted during His ministry. The Bible says, *"He is despised and rejected by men, a Man of sorrows and acquainted with grief"* (Isaiah 53:3). Jesus understands what it's like to be harassed and persecuted for fulfilling a divine purpose. The apostle Paul was also persecuted. He wrote to the Corinthians that he had been *"in stripes above measure, in prisons more frequently, in deaths often"* (2 Corinthians 11:23).

The opposition of the enemy comes when we begin to live out our purpose. However, purpose will always triumph over any opposition. In my life, I have been misunderstood and persecuted for preaching the truths of the kingdom of God, for ministering spiritual deliverance, for emphasizing the fatherhood of God, for defending and raising up the ministry of women, and so much more. While this has been hard and painful, it has not stopped me. In all such situations, my purpose has prevailed over the persecution. Nothing the enemy did, does, or will do can stop God's purpose. The Lord's plans will always be stronger than Satan's attacks.

If anyone has plans to thwart God's will or go against His children, they should know that God Himself will be their greatest opponent! Paul experienced this reality before his conversion. He was confronted by a resurrected and ascended Jesus while traveling on the road to Damascus to persecute Christians, with the goal of imprisoning and even killing them for teaching about Christ. (See Acts 9:1–2.) Paul, who was called Saul at the time of his encounter with Jesus, later spoke about that life-changing moment:

> *I saw a light from heaven, brighter than the sun, shining around me and those who journeyed with me. And when we all had fallen to the ground, I heard a voice speaking to me and saying in the Hebrew language, "Saul, Saul, why are you persecuting Me? It is hard for you to kick against the goads."* (Acts 26:13–14)

God's purpose was that Paul would be saved and bring the gospel to both Gentiles and Jews, and His purpose triumphed over all of Paul's man-made plans. No matter what you are facing—disappointment, temptation, accusation, or persecution—as long as you are living in your purpose, the successful completion of your calling is inevitable.

MORE POWERFUL THAN DEATH

Walking according to our purpose will also preserve us from untimely death because we will not die until we have fulfilled our destiny. For example, the Scriptures say, "*Now when David had served God's purpose in his own generation, he fell asleep; he was buried with his ancestors*" (Acts 13:36 NIV). In another example, Jesus was protected from premature death because He was fully aligned with His purpose. The Bible says that when Jesus was still a young child, King Herod sent orders to kill all children two years of age and under, in an attempt to destroy the Messiah who had been born in Bethlehem, but even after Herod had cruelly murdered many infants, he was not able to achieve this goal. (See Matthew 2.)

Also, there were times during Jesus's ministry when people wanted to kill Him, but they could not succeed. (See, for example, Luke 4:24–30; John 10:31–39.) Jesus died at just the right time in the plan of His Father, willingly giving up His life for us. (See John 10:15–18.) And, in fulfillment of His purpose, Jesus defeated death forever by taking our sins upon Himself on the cross, and then rising victoriously

TRUE PURPOSE ATTRACTS THE RICH RESOURCES OF THE KINGDOM.

from the dead, *"the firstborn among many brethren"* (Romans 8:29). Now, we no longer need to fear death. We have been given eternal life in Jesus. And one day, we will be physically raised from the dead, and live forever in a resurrected body. *"That through death* [Jesus] *might destroy him who had the power of death, that is, the devil, and release those who through fear of death were all their lifetime subject to bondage"* (Hebrews 2:14–15).

In my own life, I have faced various forms of danger. For example, I have been assaulted, thieves have chased me down to rob me and then held me at gunpoint, and someone even came to my church with the intention of ending my life, but they could not touch me. I have preached in countries that are very dangerous for Christians—where the gospel is forbidden, believers suffer persecution, and pastors have been put in prison or killed—but God has always preserved my life because I continue to fulfill my purpose on earth. He will do the same for you.

ACTIVATING THE POWER OF PURPOSE

As we conclude this chapter, please pray this prayer out loud to release the power of purpose in your life:

> Heavenly Father, I thank You for the revelation of these many facets of the power of purpose. Today, I activate that power and declare that I will have innovative ideas that will change the status quo in my territory and sphere of influence. I commit to remain faithful to my purpose and Your principles, to extend Your kingdom, and to give You the glory. Illuminate my mind and heart with heaven's ideas, with the thoughts You had when You created me. Reveal to me the ideas and the means that I must use to release the power connected with my purpose. I want to be known in heaven and have the ability to defeat the enemy of my soul. I don't want to be just "one of the bunch." I want my life to be guided by the calling for

which You created me so I can make positive changes in my generation. I give You thanks because I know that I will see Your power manifested as I fulfill my purpose. In Jesus's name, amen.

GOD'S PURPOSE IS MORE POWERFUL THAN OUR PLANS,
AND PREVAILS OVER THEM.

TESTIMONIES OF FINDING AND FULFILLING PURPOSE

FROM FOLLOWER OF SPIRITUALISM TO TEACHER OF THE WORD

For thirty years, Susie lived in oppression from her involvement in Santeria and spiritualism, until she was nearly killed by the spirits she served. Then, Jesus came into her life, saved her, and led her to know and fulfill her true purpose.

> I was born in Cuba but moved to the United States when I was ten years old. My mother had grown up practicing Santeria and spiritualism, and I grew up practicing these beliefs as well. From an early age, I could see and perceive the spiritual activity around me. Although I followed all the rituals, spells, and ceremonies of my mother's religion, I always had the feeling that something was missing. It was not until I was in my thirties, after having had three children and going through a horrible divorce, which left me in a state of total emptiness, that I began to look for what was missing in my life. Then, during a ceremony to devote myself to a deity I planned to serve, something unexpected happened.
>
> A demon manifested itself through one of the "santeras" present, saying that he had been sent to kill me. My mother and others who were there began to negotiate with the demon, trying to convince him not to hurt me. That was scary! For years, those spirits had been my guides and companions, and I could not understand what was happening. Full of fear, I ran to hide where I couldn't hear the demon's threats. There, I heard a soft voice that captivated me and flooded me with a peace I had never experienced before. This voice told me, "That's not what I have for you."

I gave up my parents' religion and received Jesus as my Lord and Savior, which was the most wonderful experience of my life. My eyes were opened and my broken heart was healed.

Three months after receiving Jesus, I had a beautiful vision in which He freed me from a dungeon, broke my chains, and led me through a huge forest. He urged me to run without looking back, telling me that demons were coming for me. At one point, He stopped, raised His sword, and gave the order to an army of angels to fight against the demons. He kept telling me, "Don't look back. Look forward and keep walking with Me." Then, in this vision, Jesus left me at a church, saying, "I put you here because you have to grow and heal. Never leave the church, because if you do, you will die."

At the time, I did not know what the vision meant, but little by little, I began to understand. During the first years of my Christian life, the Lord trained me in His Word. I learned to hear His voice and understand the role of the Holy Spirit. Because of my upbringing, I had many spiritual burdens and misconceptions. I needed to be renewed in my mind, break self-imposed generational curses, and heal my emotions from so many years of abuse.

WITHOUT PURPOSE, YOUR PLANS WILL NOT BE EFFECTIVE; YOU WILL BE LIKE A BIRD TRYING TO LIVE IN THE ENVIRONMENT OF A FISH.

I was determined to do whatever it took to reach my destiny in God. Being molded into the image of Christ was the hardest thing I had to go through. It took time and perseverance to learn to deny myself and achieve total surrender. But through that process, God become more real to me every day. He began to reveal His heart to me, and He placed His own love for people inside me. I started to have a burning desire to be used to free others who were in spiritual captivity. My knowledge of the occult gave me the ability to recognize the devil's tactics and identify people who were bound or enslaved to sin.

Although I had a great passion to help set people free from demons, I wasn't sure how to do it. Then, after fifteen years of dreaming of being used by God in this way, the Holy Spirit guided me to King Jesus Ministry. There, I began to learn about inner healing and deliverance, and I discovered a passion for teaching the Word of God. In one of the first deliverances in which I participated, there was a young woman who had once been involved in witchcraft. By a word of knowledge from the Holy Spirit, I knew the reason why she still lived in bondage, even though she no longer practiced witchcraft. She'd had an abortion after becoming pregnant by a man belonging to that hidden religion. As soon as I began to cast out the demon, it manifested itself in her body with great force and violence. But God set her free, and today she is happy, serving the Lord in the church and continually bearing fruit for the kingdom of God.

I remember another woman who was strongly demon-possessed as a result of having been in the occult. The Holy Spirit guided me to minister God's love as a means of deliverance. This woman told me, "I came here bound, but thanks to you showing me so much love, I was able to understand that I am the daughter of God, and I no longer have to live in oppression." In the following months, I noticed a big change in her.

Although I had been in Christ for years and finally knew what I had been called to do, I still needed to go through a process of maturing in my character and learning to die to my will, my abilities, and even my dreams. I also had to learn discipline, respect, humility, and—most importantly—that I didn't need to justify or defend myself.

Almost twenty-five years after receiving Christ into my heart, having gone through the wonderful process of being healed, delivered, and prepared by God, I was ordained as a teacher by Apostle Guillermo Maldonado. He saw the call of God on my life, and he believed in me when no one else had. Today, I know the challenges, crises, and even disappointments that come from ministering God's love to His people. But I also know that I have been called to fulfill my purpose in Him.

TRUE LEADERS DO NOT GIVE UP BECAUSE THEY ARE COMMITTED TO THEIR PURPOSE.

FROM A WHEELCHAIR TO MINISTERING HEALTH AND HEALING

Dr. Don Colbert, from Tupelo, Mississippi, suffered a massive heat stroke while he was in medical school that left him critically ill and in a wheelchair. Yet after several months, the power of his purpose enabled him to walk again. Now, he teaches God's people about divine health and healing.

> I have been a certified family doctor for over twenty-five years, and I can testify that God has done great things in my life. I have seen Him use my knowledge to teach people about their health and change the way they think and act so they can become well and whole. It is not enough for us to believe in miracles, because what we can do, God will not do. I know that God has called me to live for this purpose: to teach the body of Christ to do their part to walk in divine health and to trust God for healing. Thanks to Him, I have been able to actively pursue my purpose in this world, impacting others in my sphere of influence. As a result, thousands of people have been empowered to improve their lives.
>
> I became a doctor because I've always had a passion for learning about health. However, I had to overcome several obstacles in order to walk in my purpose. One of those hurdles occurred while I was in my third year of medical school. Here is how I described the circumstances in my book *Stress Less*:
>
>> While running a 3-mile run in 95-degree weather, with almost 100 percent humidity, I suffered a massive heat stroke. My body temperature reached 108 degrees Fahrenheit.
>>
>> I was rushed to a hospital emergency room where I received intravenous fluids. My leg muscles were

literally bursting, however—the medical condition is called rhabdomyolysis. I watched as my legs withered before my eyes. The pain was excruciating.

I was hospitalized for two to three weeks so I could receive massive amounts of intravenous fluids and be monitored for kidney failure. I began urinating coffee-colored urine from the muscle breakdown, and I was so weak that I eventually was forced to use a wheelchair.

Rather than improving, my condition grew worse as my leg muscles continued to deteriorate in spite of all the treatments. A surgeon was called in to perform a muscle biopsy. This revealed extensive muscle necrosis—in other words, muscle cell death. I was told I would probably never walk again. By this time, my arms actually appeared larger than my legs.

I felt under extreme stress. I had missed more than a month of medical school, and now I was being told I would probably never walk again!

I needed a miracle, and I received one. After a couple of months of rest

PURPOSE CARRIES THE POWER OF GOD TO OVERCOME ALL OPPOSITION.

> and a lot of prayer, I was able to walk again. Miraculously I regained the strength as well as the size of my leg muscles.[3]

Thanks to the prayers of many people and my wife's affirmation that God was going to heal me, a miracle happened. It would have been very difficult for me to inspire and teach people about health if I hadn't overcome this serious medical condition. It was my biggest challenge in life, but by the grace of God, I was healed. I marvel at what He has done in my life since then, enabling me to fulfill my purpose of teaching people about healthy living. I do this through my medical practice and the avenues of publishing, seminars, media appearances, and nutritional products. I have written more than forty books and am a *New York Times* best-selling author. Together, my books have sold millions of copies. All the glory goes to God for healing me, teaching me about divine health, and allowing me to share what I've learned with others.

3. Don Colbert, MD, *Stress Less* (Lake Mary, FL: Siloam, 2005), 1–2.

INDICATORS OF PURPOSE

GOD HAS DESIGNED EACH OF US IN A PARTICULAR WAY THAT PROVIDES INDICATORS OF OUR PURPOSE.

8

INDICATORS OF PURPOSE

At the beginning of this book, we looked at some of the most common questions every human being asks: "Who am I?" "Where do I come from?" "Why am I here?" "Where am I going?" We know that we are God's beloved children who have been created in His image and likeness. God has given us a specific purpose, and we have to learn what that purpose is. When we discover our calling and enter into it, we can fulfill the reason for our existence on earth.

Abraham and his wife, Sarah, had no offspring, and Sarah was beyond the age of bearing a child. But God had given Abraham a promise that he would be the ancestor of multitudes, and when it was time for that purpose to unfold, the Lord gave Sarah the ability to conceive and bear a son by Abraham. When this happened, not only did the history of this one family change, but the history of God's people changed forever. (See Genesis 17–18:15; 21:1–7.)

Jesus was known as the son of Joseph the carpenter until the season came for Him to enter into the main purpose for His life. After Jesus was baptized, the heavens opened and God the Father presented Him before the world, saying, "*This is My beloved Son, in whom I am well pleased"* (Matthew 3:17). Jesus's purpose of redeeming humanity changed the history of the world.

How will your life change when you enter into your destiny? How will your calling transform the world for the kingdom of God?

As long as we don't know the answers to essential questions like those listed above, we will feel adrift in life and be unable to fulfill our purpose. However, as we obtain the answers, our life will become meaningful and full. Therefore, now that you understand many aspects of the nature and power of purpose, I want to help you identify the main calling of your life so you can enter into it. We cannot recognize it through our intellect alone; rather, it is revealed and confirmed to us by the Holy Spirit. Nonetheless, God has designed each of us in a particular way that provides indicators of our purpose. These are like unique seals of the destiny that God designated for our life before the foundation of the world. The following are some of these indicators.

HOLY FRUSTRATION

Jesus spent the first thirty years of His life observing the blind, the deaf, and the lame. However, because it was not yet His season to begin His ministry, He was unable to heal them. I'm sure He must have felt some degree of frustration over this because inside of Him burned a fire to heal and deliver people. I call such a feeling "holy frustration." Those who feel a holy frustration in the face of the injustice,

ONLY TWO THINGS CAN STOP A PURPOSE, AND BOTH DEPEND ON US: DISBELIEF AND DISOBEDIENCE.

poverty, ignorance, immaturity, sickness, depression, mental illness, marital breakdown, and other issues and problems in the world cannot stay the same. Their frustration is an indication of their true purpose, which prompts them to bring positive change to individuals and society. At age thirty, when His season arrived, what if Jesus had not responded to His holy frustration and followed His divine purpose, but instead remained a carpenter all His life? We never would have known Him as Messiah and Lord, and He never would have gone to the cross to become our Savior. We would still be lost in our sins. And who knows what the state of the world would be right now?

Moses grew up in Egypt as the adopted son of Pharaoh's daughter, but he knew something about his Hebrew background. His holy frustration was evident when he saw an Egyptian beating a Hebrew and identified with the one who was being oppressed. Moses realized he wanted to do something to protect and help his own people. The next day, when he saw two Hebrews fighting, he was distressed at their animosity toward one another. He was frustrated that they weren't living in unity. With these reactions, he was reflecting his divine call to free the Hebrews from slavery and draw them together as one people under God. (See Exodus 2:1–13.)

HOLY ANGER

Another indicator of your purpose is "holy anger." Let's return to the example of Moses. Anger may have been the first sign of his purpose, even before his frustration. "*Now it came to pass in those days, when Moses was grown, that he went out to his brethren and looked at their burdens. And he saw an Egyptian beating a Hebrew, one of his brethren. So he looked this way and that way, and when he saw no one, he killed the Egyptian and hid him in the sand*" (Exodus 2:11–12). As contradictory as it might seem, this incident was the beginning of Moses's purpose. Did he do wrong? Of course! He shouldn't have killed the Egyptian. Yet his purpose was to end Egypt's abuse and slavery of the people of God. The anger he felt when he saw the mistreatment of one of his people was an indicator of his calling in life.

However, Moses's immediate reaction to the injustice he witnessed is a caution for us. This is an example of taking our holy frustration and anger into our own hands and not waiting for God to direct us in how to fulfill our purpose. It would take forty years of living in the desert for Moses to be prepared to free his brothers from slavery. But when he was ready, God did miraculous works through him on behalf of His people, and Moses fulfilled his purpose. (See Exodus 2–3.) Thus, when you experience holy frustration and anger, take your concerns to God and ask Him to guide you in how best to respond to them.

What makes you angry? What situation do you want to change? Anger turns into holy indignation when we have the ability to focus our anointing, efforts, and faith on an issue, with the aim of producing transformation. When this happens, we are ready to move forward with our purpose. It is when we say, "Enough is enough!" and start working on making that change. In my case, it makes me angry to see disease robbing people of health; it makes me angry to see so many people bound by curses, including those produced by the very words of their mouths. I am also angered by poverty and by ignorance of the Word of God. My anger about these conditions has shown me I have been called to change them. God

A HOLY FRUSTRATION WILL PROMPT YOU TO SEEK YOUR TRUE PURPOSE IN LIFE.

has anointed me to bring freedom and transformation in all of these areas.

THE IDEAS THAT OCCUPY YOUR MIND

When people have their mind set on the flesh, or the sinful nature, then their mind becomes an enemy of God, and any thoughts about their purpose in Him disappear. (See Romans 8:5–8.) The Bible warns, *"But in accordance with your hardness and your impenitent heart you are treasuring up for yourself wrath in the day of wrath and revelation of the righteous judgment of God"* (Romans 2:5). In contrast, the Scriptures teach us the right way of thinking: *"Finally, brethren, whatever things are true, whatever things are noble, whatever things are just, whatever things are pure, whatever things are lovely, whatever things are of good report, if there is any virtue and if there is anything praiseworthy—meditate on these things"* (Philippians 4:8). Once you set your mind in the right direction, it will be like a ship sailing toward its destination.

Therefore, when your mind ceases to be at enmity with God, thoughts about your purpose will predominate. From that point on, selfish thoughts will diminish, and you will start focusing on the needs of others. You will find that ideas related to your purpose are always with you, whether you are awake or asleep, because they are linked to your purpose.

What ideas occupy your mind? Do you find yourself thinking about matters relating to the family, ministry, business, justice, education, or medicine? You should start paying attention to your thought patterns, because they will help reveal your purpose. Thought produces action, and repeated or persistent action creates a habit. There are both good and bad habits, but all good habits are related to purpose.

A WRONG THAT MOVES PEOPLE TO ACTION IS WHAT THEY ARE CALLED TO CHANGE.

A DESIRE TO PURSUE A PARTICULAR ENDEAVOR

Similar to the previous point, whatever you continually seek out or diligently pursue is an indicator of your purpose. What have you been chasing all of your life? What would you still like to achieve? Is it a type of ministry? A business? A particular vocation? Consider what you reach toward most in both your thoughts and actions.

A PARTICULAR COMPASSION FOR OTHERS

We have noted how Moses, after seeing a fellow Hebrew being beaten by an Egyptian, felt moved by the fate of his brother. This was because his life calling was to free his people from slavery and oppression. Jesus was moved to compassion by the state of people's lives as He toured cities and villages and taught in their synagogues. The Scriptures say, "*When He saw the multitudes, He was moved with compassion for them, because they were weary and scattered, like sheep having no shepherd*" (Matthew 9:36). We can learn to discern God's purpose for us by what moves us to compassion.

A HOLY PASSION

Whatever awakens a "holy passion" within you is another indicator of your purpose. It is a burning desire, an internal fire that never goes out. For many people, any feeling or display of passion is offensive, so they tend to ignore their God-given passion and practice "casual Christianity" instead. However, God is pouring out on this generation the fire of His Holy Spirit, which releases a consuming passion for divine purpose.

Such passion produces a strong motivation to be or do something in life. Remember how Jeremiah had a passion that consumed him? *"Then I said, 'I will not make mention of Him, nor speak anymore in His name.' But His word was in my heart like a burning fire shut up in my bones; I was weary of holding it back, and I could not"* (Jeremiah 20:9). Jeremiah's purpose was to warn the people about the divine judgment that was coming, and he wanted them to repent of their sin against God.

To have passion is to accept pain in our lives, because passion involves being willing to face disappointments, experience weariness and suffering, and even give our lives for our purpose. Jesus fully embraced His purpose, and He was willing to suffer the unspeakable in order to fulfill it. His surrendering His life for us is commonly known as "the passion of Christ," referring to all of the pain He endured to become our Savior. The Bible tells us about other passionate men as well. Moses's passion was to be in the presence of God and speak with Him face-to-face. Joshua's passion was to fight until God's people had conquered the promised land. David's passion was to worship the one true God with all his might. John the Baptist's passion was to prepare the way for the Messiah. Paul's passion was to preach the gospel to the Gentiles.

Although it is essential for us to have a passion for our purpose, we must be careful not to allow that passion to become obsession. Passion leads us to be focused on what we need to do, and this is necessary because it enables us to persevere and be effective in fulfilling our calling. Obsession is a perversion of passion that creates fanaticism, produces isolation, hurts people, and causes destruction because it does not come from God. Always seek to be directed by the Lord in your passion and monitor your thoughts and actions by the fruit of the Spirit. (See Galatians 5:22–23.)

A SENSE OF ACCOMPLISHMENT AND FULFILLMENT

If you are motivated to do something in particular, and it gives you a feeling of accomplishment, this is a further indicator of your purpose. When your work or any other activity does not lead to a sense of fulfillment, that is a sign you are not in your purpose. Start observing the activities in your life that cause you to feel fulfilled. What activity fills your heart with joy?

The most miserable person isn't the one who has no money or job. It's the person who is involved in work or activities that have nothing to do with their purpose. On the other hand, the happiest person is the one who—regardless of the amount of sacrifice they must go through, the degree of suffering they experience, or how much people misunderstand them—is working on their calling. The individual who is living according to their purpose feels fulfilled, happy, and "just right" for what they are doing.

A DIVINE BURDEN

I define a "divine burden" as an obligation that leads us to perform an action. It is a situation that we cannot bear, and feel we must resolve. We take it on and do not stop until we have done something about it. For example, if you see people living on the street, without any food to eat, and you feel that you need to help remedy this situation, you have identified your purpose of helping the homeless. If you

WHEN YOUR MIND IS CLEAR OF SINFUL THOUGHTS, IT BEGINS TO FOCUS ON THOUGHTS OF PURPOSE.

see people who don't know God, and you feel you have do something to show them the way to the Father, you have identified your purpose of teaching or evangelizing. If you see people who are sick, and you feel that you cannot just leave them in that state, then you have identified your purpose of being in the medical profession or exercising the gift of healing or miracles. If you see the devastation that results from broken homes, and you feel you must bring hope in such situations, then you have identified your purpose of restoring families.

What burdens you? Is it your children's future, governmental corruption, the poor, the sick, the oppressed, dysfunctional families, a lack of direction in the lives of youth, people's ignorance about right and wrong, people's psychological or emotional suffering, people's need to know Christ, the rights of unborn children, or something else? If you identify your divine burden, you will identify your purpose.

SUPERNATURAL GRACE TO ACCOMPLISH SOMETHING

We need to diligently pursue whatever is in the realm of our purpose, but we don't have to strive to do it because we will receive God's supernatural grace for it. If there is a task that is generally considered difficult, but you find easy to do, this means that you are working in the supernatural grace of God. I call this "the grace factor." Paul said, *"But by the grace of God I am what I am, and His grace toward me was not in vain; but I labored more abundantly than they all, yet not I, but the grace of God which was with me"* (1 Corinthians 15:10).

The grace factor is not the same as "situational grace," which comes at a given time for a specific purpose. In the Old Testament, we read about a donkey that prophesied once, but that doesn't mean the donkey was a prophet. (See Numbers 22:21–40.) We should not base our life's purpose on something that happened to us once, or even happens to us occasionally. Grace that is related to our purpose works in a similar way as the previous indicators. When God's anointing, grace, and power *continually* come upon you with regard to the same activity, it is an indicator that you have identified your life purpose.

LOOK FOR THE INDICATORS

As we conclude this chapter, I encourage you to carefully consider all of the above indicators of purpose. Pray that you will be able to recognize the specific indicators of your unique calling and begin to walk toward the glorious destiny God has for you.

> Lord Jesus, I believe that You have a purpose for my life and have delineated my destiny on this earth. I want to find and follow Your purpose. I ask that You would reveal it to my spirit so I can fulfill my calling. Help me to recognize the indicators that show me this purpose. Give me the courage to go through Your process of being prepared for my destiny, and not to give up in the face of adversity or opposition. Help me to see Your destiny for my life in what frustrates me, angers me, or ignites passion within me. Please give me Your grace and anointing so I can be filled with Your power. I desire to make a difference in this world in my generation. I want to manifest Your glory in my sphere of influence and not just "serve time" but truly live for a purpose. I want my life to

OUR DOMINANT THOUGHTS AND POSITIVE HABITS SPEAK OF OUR PURPOSE; THEY ARE A PATTERN OF IDEAS AND ACTIONS RELATING TO WHAT WE ARE CALLED TO DO.

have an impact and leave a legacy for the next generation. Here I am, Lord—use me! Amen.

TESTIMONIES OF FINDING AND FULFILLING PURPOSE

AN UNFOLDING PURPOSE IN THE MIDST OF CRISES

Apostle José Luis López was an architect and his wife, Prophet Margarita Palmer, was a lawyer when they changed course and began their ministry in Mexico. After they connected with the vision of King Jesus Ministry, they began to see an increase in God's activity in their life and ministry. They have faced natural and spiritual opposition, but have overcome it. Today, their congregation has more than twenty-five thousand people, and it continues to grow.

> We both had professional careers, but we always knew that God had called us to serve in ministry. Making the transition was not easy, but our passion for ministry was always greater than the difficulties we encountered. Everything we went through directed us to our divine purpose. In 1991, we started by sharing our faith with family and friends because we felt a burden for them. Although we knew that God had called us to transform Mexico, we understood that we first had to work for the salvation of our own relatives. During the first years, about fifty people attended our church. Then, when we placed ourselves under the covering of King Jesus Ministry, we found ourselves on a direct path to our purpose and destiny and began to see an exponential growth of believers

WHAT STIRS YOUR COMPASSION IS AN INDICATOR OF YOUR PURPOSE.

and leadership. However, we faced many challenges that were beyond our control.

In late October and early November 2007, Tabasco, the state in which we live in Mexico, suffered some of the worst floods in our country's history, leaving more than half of our capital's population with their homes underwater, and five of the seventeen municipalities in the state flooded as well, with up to about twenty feet of water. The church building was under more than eight feet of water. Everything was underwater! In the midst of this chaos and a move to a new location, we sheltered whole families who had been affected, and we gathered our church members in the Houses of Peace that were still active after the flood. A House of Peace is a home in which people meet weekly to hear the Word and receive miracles from God in their lives. The meetings are led by leaders trained in our church. We had hundreds of these Houses of Peace, thanks to the vision of King Jesus. In December of that year, with the city still flooded, we hosted a "Houses of Peace Celebration" in which we opened our doors and ministered to eight thousand people, five thousand of whom had never attended before. Thus, our greatest ministerial explosion occurred in the midst of the biggest crisis and chaos that our city had ever gone through.

In 2009, a pandemic of the H1N1 influenza virus emerged nationwide, and as part of the contagion control, the government banned mass meetings. Again, God's strategy was to work through the Houses of Peace. At that time, the most remarkable testimonies began to emerge. Entire families accepted Jesus, there were conversions of gang members, individuals who were on the verge of suicide were saved, and people with all kinds of diseases were healed. The number of attendees at the Houses of Peace doubled during the quarantine.

GOD-GIVEN PASSION CANNOT BE CONTAINED; IT BREAKS LOOSE WHEN WE KNOW AND RECEIVE OUR PURPOSE.

We also witnessed our city collapse financially due to the fall of the oil industry. All economic activity diminished, and insecurity increased. The city, one of the most violent in the country, was desolate because many families had left our state as a result of a wave of kidnappings and a lack of employment. But we did not give up because our passion for our purpose was greater than these calamities. We felt a holy anger against the tricks of the enemy to bring us down. When we prayed and fasted, God began to manifest powerful financial miracles among the members of our congregation. Supernaturally, million-dollar contracts began to be signed, huge debts were canceled, and our ministry continued to grow.

We currently have daughter churches and coverage in almost half of Mexico (in fourteen of the thirty-two states), and in nations such as Guatemala, Honduras, and Argentina. God has used us to impact our nation. During the most recent Supernatural Encounter in the Mexico City Arena, we registered 3,100 people who received Christ and documented 1,033 miracles and healings.

One of the testimonies that struck us the most was that of a pastor who had a serious health condition in which his left lung was full of gaps due to a bacterium. His doctor had told him that he should not travel to

Mexico City because the altitude would cause his lung to collapse. This man couldn't walk, much less run. But by faith, he came to the encounter, and when we prayed for him, God performed a miracle and healed him! I also remember a woman who came with a life-threatening disorder called placenta percreta, "a condition where the placenta attaches itself and grows through the uterus and potentially to the nearby organs (such as the bladder)."[4] It is the most severe form of a complication that occurs in one in 2500 women, and one person in three dies from it.[5] The woman's ailment was so severe that she'd undergone surgery to remove her womb and part of her bladder, and she had four hundred stitches! The doctors had given her no hope. However, at the encounter, the fire of God came upon her, and when a leader placed her hand on the woman's abdomen, she felt the organs re-form. In our ministry, there have also been many testimonies similar to what happened when one of our youth ministers prayed, through the phone, for a woman who had been dead for fifteen minutes, and in the presence of paramedics, the dead person vomited and came back to life.

Each situation has been a great challenge of faith, but God has brought us from glory to glory and used us for His divine purposes. Thanks to the vision of King Jesus Ministry and our apostle, Guillermo Maldonado, we have been able to see how all our obstacles have ended in victory, because purpose is stronger than any opposition. Through King Jesus Ministry, God has connected us to our purpose and used us to link others to what He is pouring out in these end times.

---

4. See https://www.brighamandwomens.org/obgyn/maternal-fetal-medicine/pregnancy-complications/placenta-accreta.

5. See https://www.ncbi.nlm.nih.gov/pmc/articles/PMC2777065/.

WE CAN RECOGNIZE OUR PURPOSE BY THE TYPE OF BURDENS WE CARRY.

THE ENEMY TRIED TO ROB HIS PURPOSE

Josue is a youth pastor at King Jesus Ministry in Miami. However, when he was a teenager, he fell into rebellion, which dragged him into sexual immorality, drugs, and violence. The enemy was stealing his purpose, until God intervened.

> I am a third-generation pastor. I grew up going to church and Sunday school, having devotions with my parents, and reading the Bible. I was a firm believer in Jesus, but suddenly, I fell into a state of rebellion that caused tumult in my life. I started going out to nightclubs and returning home drunk, on drugs, and even having been in shootings. My life was a constant party of sex and alcohol. The rebellion consumed me, and I didn't look at the consequences of my actions. I went from thinking that I would never respond badly to my parents, to fighting with them and making my mother afraid of me. I went from believing that I would marry a virgin to living a promiscuous lifestyle, and from being a quiet child to getting involved in gangs and violence. My parents were unable to control me, and I did not receive correction from anyone. The rebellion stole my innocence.
>
> Even though I had grown up in a Christian church, it was a church without the presence and power of the Holy Spirit. Then I went to

King Jesus Ministry. I remember attending retreats and having encounters with God, but due to the pressure of my friends, I didn't fully surrender my life back to God. When I was nineteen, I went to a retreat that marked and changed me forever. Although I returned to my old friends in the world, I was now the only one among them who didn't drink alcohol. Gradually, I lost interest in my rebellious lifestyle, and I started to invite my friends to church. I began to die to my past, to old friendships, and to the worldly atmosphere. I was no longer the same.

The process was continuous, yet long and slow. One day, after a fistfight outside the church, instead of leaving, I entered the church, and that day, God freed me from anger and cigarette addiction. He continued to change areas of my life that I could not change on my own. At King Jesus, I was placed under a mentor, but I still didn't want anyone to correct me or preach to me, so I avoided him all the time. If an usher wanted to change my seat, I refused or threatened to hit him. I would watch the preachers and then tell God that I didn't want to be like them, talking about God all day. I had no idea of the plans the Lord had for me!

Despite the rebellion that was still in me, I grew in discipleship, vision, and the Word. I began to respond to God's presence by committing myself more and more each time. One day, when I was supposed to be at a House of Peace meeting, I went with an ex-girlfriend to have sex at a certain place, but when we arrived there, the conviction of the Holy Spirit made me leave and go to the meeting instead. There, I was given a prophetic word about my purpose. That changed me and encouraged me to give everything to God completely. One night, thanks to my mentor's example, I began to have an intimate relationship with

WE ARE SUCCESSFUL WHEN WE KNOW GOD'S PURPOSE AND LEAVE A LEGACY ON EARTH.

God on my own, in addition to what I was doing at the church, and I promised to pray daily.

Then, I started to see a massive breakthrough in my life. Everything accelerated, and I began to be hungry for the fire of God. I dedicated myself to winning souls and developed a great passion for the Lord. I wanted to live and die for Him! I started asking God, "What is my purpose? Why am I alive? Why am I here?" I realized that I seemed to be the only one at the church who didn't manifest a gift. Some people sang, others played instruments, and most people did something or other, but I had nothing specific to contribute. I felt as if God had forgotten me in that respect. So, I started calling all my friends from the past to bring them to Christ. I became a House of Peace leader and an evangelist in the streets, and I got closer to my mentor and leaders. I changed my environment and those who I associated with, and God revealed my purpose through the people around me at the church.

At that time, my House of Peace grew so much that I had to hold meetings in two shifts. I liked to preach and talk about God all the time. I began to love His Word and wanted to share His message. I had a passion to win souls and to serve anyone, in any way, whether it was other people, my leaders, or my spiritual father. I learned to trust the voice of God and that of my leaders.

Every aspect of the vision of King Jesus has helped me to become what I am today. Five years ago, Apostle Maldonado called me to lead the youth, and I went through another very hard process of humility, surrender, and maturation. I remember a word that the apostle gave me about my destiny. He told me that I would spend a few more years at home, raising up others and multiplying the fruit, and then be sent to the nations, where I would fill stadiums. After I received that word, I endured a season of much rejection and criticism from people; some who had been close to me turned against me. I had to face false accusations, manipulation, and division, and I dealt with a fear of man. There were young people who arrived at the church in the same state of rebellion that I had been in at the beginning, and now I had to pay the price to form them. It was the toughest season of my life. It got to the point where I wanted to leave everything, but by the grace of God, I was able to persevere in my duties and service to Him. The fire for my purpose was greater than these troubles.

I believe that the key is obedience, commitment, perseverance, and taking responsibility for God's dreams for our lives. Now, my wife and I see how the lives of so many people are impacted by what God is doing through us. We are eager to see what God will do next!

HOW TO
DISCOVER YOUR PURPOSE

WHEN WE HAVE INTIMATE COMMUNION WITH GOD, HE MAKES US HIS FRIEND.

9

HOW TO DISCOVER YOUR PURPOSE

If we want to know our purpose, we must go to the Source—to the Person who created us, and that Person is God. God's Holy Spirit is the One who reveals His mysteries to us, and if we are hungry to discover our purpose in life, He is willing to disclose it.

Remember, purpose is not discovered naturally. There is a significant difference between the process of discovering and the process of receiving revelation. Discovering involves acquiring knowledge through studies, research, experiments, statistics, and so on. It also refers to seeking out what is unknown. Receiving revelation, on the other hand, is a supernatural process in which our spiritual senses are opened and our understanding is enlightened to see the truth of who we are and the purpose of our existence.

When we receive revelation, the human mind does not do the work. Instead, knowledge that comes directly from God is given to us by the Holy Spirit. The Scriptures tell us, *"However, when He, the Spirit of truth, has come, He will guide you into all truth; for He will not speak on His own authority, but whatever He hears He will speak; and He will tell you things to come"* (John 16:13). As we have seen, God does give us indicators of our purpose, which involve natural processes of observing and analyzing, but we must set those indicators alongside the revelation of His purpose for us in order to confirm our calling.

This process of receiving revelation is vital for us to understand because many people confuse the purpose of their life with the profession for which they prepared in college or trade school. Although the two may well coincide, education is a function of the natural realm, while purpose, although it operates in the natural, has spiritual characteristics, and its effect is supernatural and eternal. Therefore, education may prepare us for a job, but it does not prepare us for a purpose.

RECEIVING REVEALED KNOWLEDGE

How does the revelation of God's purpose come to us? The Holy Spirit uses supernatural means, such as a dream, a vision, the audible voice of God, a sign, a supernatural encounter, or a prophetic word. The Spirit chooses the way in which He reveals our purpose, and it is different for each person.

God's Spirit can show us the purpose of our life because He understands it completely. He knows what the Father had in mind when He created us. He is the very Spirit of the Creator Himself, and He exercises God's creative power.

> *For the Spirit searches all things, yes, the deep things of God. For what man knows the things of a man except the spirit of the man which is*

THE FIRST REVELATION WE RECEIVE LEADS US TO RECOGNIZE JESUS AS OUR SAVIOR. WE LEARN OUR PURPOSE THROUGH OUR RELATIONSHIP WITH HIM.

> *in him? Even so no one knows the things of God except the Spirit of God. Now we have received...the Spirit who is from God, that we might know the things that have been freely given to us by God.*
> (1 Corinthians 2:10–12)

The Holy Spirit is in charge of revealing our unique, unrepeatable, and eternal purpose. Is there anything we can do to cooperate with Him in the revelation of this purpose? Can we prepare our spiritual senses to be open to receiving His knowledge? Yes, we can! Here are some vital guidelines for doing so.

KNOW GOD

No one can know their purpose without first knowing God. When we know Him, we find out who we are, and we turn our hearts toward His purposes. We need to seek the Lord because aligning ourselves with the one true God is the only way we can really understand what we were created for. We must dedicate time and effort to knowing Him better, to understanding His plans and our role in them.

When we truly know God, we stop questioning and resisting His will for us. Whoever questions the voice of God has a problem because they are not in harmony with His heart and mind. Jesus said, *"My sheep hear my voice, and I know them, and they follow Me"* (John 10:27). With this metaphor of sheep, the Lord is referring to the people who have a covenant with Him, those who know His heart, His love, and His teachings, and who obey them faithfully and wholeheartedly.

The best way to know God is to recognize His voice, and one of the means by which God speaks to us is through His written Word. In the Scriptures, God reveals who He is. He Himself inspired the Scriptures to make Himself known to mankind. (See, for example, 2 Timothy 3:16–17.) When we know God's Word, we will know Him, because His

Word tells us His nature and will. What God says about Himself and who He is are one and the same.

In addition to knowing God's Word, we need to be in continuous communion with Him through prayer, fasting, and seeking Him daily. *"The secret of the Lord is with those who fear Him, and He will show them His covenant"* (Psalm 25:14).

Abraham first entered into an intimate relationship with God when the Lord made a covenant with him, and Abraham responded in faith. God said that He would make Abraham *"a great nation,"* and that in him, *"all the families of the earth* [would] *be blessed."* (See Genesis 12:1–4.) At that time, God told Abraham to leave his father's house, customs, and gods, and walk with Him through the desert toward a land God would show Him. Later, the Lord described that land as *"flowing with milk and honey."* (See, for example, Exodus 3:8.)

On the road to receiving God's promises, Abraham dwelled near Sodom and Gomorrah, two cities that God planned to destroy because of the multitude of their iniquities. Because of the covenant He had made with Abraham, the Lord could not hide these plans from him:

> *And the Lord said, "Shall I hide from Abraham what I am doing, since Abraham shall surely become a great and mighty nation, and all the nations of the earth shall be blessed in him? For I have known him, in order that he*

WORSHIP IS A MEANS TO KNOWING GOD BECAUSE IT CAUSES HIM TO REVEAL HIMSELF TO US.

> *may command his children and his household after him, that they keep the way of the* Lord, *to do righteousness and justice, that the Lord may bring to Abraham what He has spoken to him."*
>
> (Genesis 18:17–19)

There are benefits to which we are entitled when we live in covenant with God, and one of them is to know the reason for certain plans He has made, since He does not hide His purposes from those who are close to Him. God considered Abraham His friend (see, for example, James 2:23), and therefore He did not hide from him what He was about to do.

In another biblical example, David grew in his knowledge of the Lord and developed an intimate relationship with Him while shepherding his father's sheep high in the mountains, meditating on the Scriptures and the nature of God. And with his musical instruments, he worshipped the Lord. David knew God, and God knew him, for the Lord revealed Himself to David's heart. If we want to know our purpose, we must come to know God in a deeper way, and a significant means by which we do this is by worshipping Him. Worship arises from our heart when we have and maintain a covenant relationship with God. It is during worship that He reveals Himself to us, and in that revelation comes the knowledge of our purpose. As our relationship with God grows, we will receive more revelation of our calling.

"But without faith it is impossible to please [God], *for he who comes to God must believe that He is, and that He is a rewarder of those who diligently seek Him"* (Hebrews 11:6). We must remember that God *is*—in a continuous present. He is always here and now. There is nothing He lacks in order to "be" something in the future. Most people either look to the future or dwell on the past. It is hard for them to live in the present. But God is unchanging, and He lives in a permanent now. The Scriptures declare, *"Jesus Christ is the same yesterday, today, and forever"* (Hebrews

13:8). Thus, let us go in faith now to the eternal God and receive a revelation of our purpose.

BE IN THE RIGHT ENVIRONMENT

It has been said that "we are the product of our environment," and there is a lot of truth to that statement. To fulfill our purpose, we must be in the right environment—spiritually, mentally, emotionally, physically, and geographically. If someone is in an environment that does not cultivate, nourish, or develop their purpose, they will be unable to accomplish it.

Think about the current environments in which you live, in all aspects of your life. What are you doing to prepare and adjust these environments for the nurturing of your purpose? Your preparation can range from simple matters, such as having better organization in your workspace, to greater issues, like discerning which friends and associates with whom you should spend your time. As the saying goes, "You can't soar like an eagle if you hang out with chickens!" Recognize that if you are not in the right environment, you will be hindered from achieving your purpose.

SERVE A VISION

The idea of "vision" is often defined as how *we* see our future. However, in terms of purpose, vision

WITHOUT VISION, A PURPOSE CANNOT BE SERVED BECAUSE VISION PROCESSES US FOR OUR PURPOSE.

is *God's* perspective on our future. This is what He reveals to us as we develop an intimate relationship with Him.

In the parable of the talents, the master gave his servants money to invest while he went away on a long trip. When he returned, he said to the servants who had invested his money wisely, *"Well done, good and faithful servant; you were faithful over a few things, I will make you ruler over many things. Enter into the joy of your lord"* (Matthew 25:21; see also verse 23). These servants were good stewards of their master's vision. They multiplied the talents he had given them, and when he returned from his journey, they presented him with the profits.

If we want to know our purpose, we must be committed to a vision. Whatever vision you have—whether it is to be a doctor, firefighter, scientist, builder, musician, businessman, writer, nurse, pastor, or apostle—it is almost always necessary to begin by serving the vision of someone else and being faithful in that capacity. God will not entrust us with our own vision until we first learn to be *"faithful over a few things."*

By serving someone else's vision, we can find the place of our own purpose because vision is the point where purpose begins. For example, at King Jesus Ministry, many people's purposes have been revealed and developed as they have served the vision of the church. We have raised up pastors, prophets, teachers, evangelists, and apostles. We have also drawn out the potential of worshippers, intercessors, and youth leaders, and we have helped married couples and children find their gifts. Additionally, through the church's vision, the Lord has given strategies to many people, enabling them to head toward their purpose as entrepreneurs, politicians, judges, doctors, artists, athletes, and more. As you can see, some of these purposes are directly related to ministry, while others function outside of a church setting. However, all these believers continue to grow in their callings according to the revelation of the Holy Spirit and the covering of our ministry.

We can say that our purpose reflects who we are, but our vision guides us to where we are going. I know people who have a purpose, but they have no vision for it. How can anyone reach a place if they don't know that it exists or where to find it? We must have a strong vision to be able to reach our destiny.

RECEIVE A SUPERNATURAL ENCOUNTER

We can also receive a revelation of our purpose through a supernatural encounter directly initiated by God. Here is an example from the life of Moses:

> *Now Moses was tending the flock of Jethro his father-in-law, the priest of Midian, and he led the flock to the far side of the wilderness and came to Horeb, the mountain of God. There the angel of the* Lord *appeared to him in flames of fire from within a bush. Moses saw that though the bush was on fire it did not burn up. So Moses thought, "I will go over and see this strange sight—why the bush does not burn up." When the* Lord *saw that he had gone over to look, God called to him from within the bush, "Moses! Moses!" And Moses said, "Here I am."* (Exodus 3:1–4 NIV)

The pattern we see throughout the Scriptures is that God presents Himself to His people through supernatural encounters. In those encounters, He reveals people's purposes and callings. Why did Moses need an encounter with God? Until that meeting,

TO FULFILL OUR PURPOSE, WE MUST BE IN THE RIGHT ENVIRONMENT—SPIRITUALLY, MENTALLY, EMOTIONALLY, PHYSICALLY, AND GEOGRAPHICALLY.

he hadn't understand his purpose or why he had gone through certain experiences in life. He had grown up in Egypt as the son of Pharaoh's daughter, been educated in the palace, and knew Egyptian culture. What he did not know was why he had been separated from his true family and people. Yet, in that encounter, he had a revelation of the one true God, whose name is *"I Am Who I Am"* (Exodus 3:14). As a result, Moses learned who he was and what his purpose was—to be the leader who would free God's people, the Hebrews, from bondage. After this, he was able make sense of the earlier events of his life.

A supernatural encounter makes God "real" to us. He Himself becomes the reality in which we live. After an encounter, He is more real to us than any opposition, persecution, disappointment, or even blessing. If God had not become real to me, I would have thrown in the towel long ago! Without my encounters with Him, I probably would have perished in the enemy's attacks. But now, God is more real to me than the daily circumstances of my life or any betrayal I have experienced, and I am able to rise above all difficulties.

Supernatural encounters transform your heart, reveal your purpose, and activate your calling. If you want an encounter with God, you must be hungry for Him and eager to know His purpose for you. Through encounters, God makes you a bearer of His presence, purpose, and power. Be ready to receive a divine encounter! Ask the Lord to open your spiritual senses to perceive what He wants to reveal to you.

WILL YOU ACCEPT THE CHALLENGE?

To sum up, purpose is not something we can discover by natural means; instead, it is revealed to us by our Creator. To receive this revelation, we learn to know God by developing an intimate relationship with Him, position ourselves in the right environment, start serving another person's vision, and receive a supernatural encounter initiated by Him.

Only then will we know our true self and receive our own vision. All of this involves a process that is often lengthy but has incalculable value because, through it, our character is formed and we are prepared to be successful in fulfilling our destiny in God.

Therefore, here is your challenge for this particular time in your life: Draw closer to God, seeking Him in the intimacy of prayer and worship. Submit to the process that He has prepared in order to form your character into the image of Christ. Be filled with the anointing of the Holy Spirit. And commit to live according to the purpose for which you exist on earth. The price is high and the process is hard, but the reward is to live in Christ to the fullest, be involved in the advancement of the kingdom of God, leave a legacy of blessing to subsequent generations, and be part of the remnant that prepares the way for the second coming of Christ. Will you accept this challenge?

If you are willing to receive this challenge and be part of the remnant God is looking for at this time, I invite you to pray a final prayer with me:

> Heavenly Father, I thank You for all the revelation about my purpose that You have brought into my life through this book. It is no coincidence that this teaching has crossed my path because it is part of Your plan for me. Today, I make a commitment to seek You more, to know You more intimately, and to know myself in the light of Your presence.

SUBMIT TO THE PROCESS THAT GOD HAS PREPARED IN ORDER TO FORM YOUR CHARACTER INTO THE IMAGE OF CHRIST.

I pledge to seek the right environment to maximize my potential and serve a vision given by You. I await the supernatural encounter initiated by You that will launch me in my destiny and move me toward fulfilling my purpose on earth. Here I am, Lord! I am willing to do Your will, and not my own. Grant me Your grace and power to endure all adversity and overcome all obstacles that stand in the way. I know that in You, I will do great things. I pray this in the name of Jesus—who died and rose again, who fulfilled His purpose on earth and changed history forever. Amen.

TESTIMONIES OF FINDING AND FULFILLING PURPOSE

CALLED TO WIN ROME FOR THE KINGDOM

Elena Posarelli is a former businesswoman whom the Lord has called as one of His apostles to spread the kingdom of God in Italy. When she was a young woman, she was abducted and abused. Despite this, she became a prosperous businesswoman, but she experienced other crises until God directed her to a church where she was led to a relationship with Jesus. Then, when she connected with King Jesus Ministry, she found her true life purpose.

> I was born in Florence, Italy, but I currently live in Rome. My childhood and adolescence were difficult due to the way my stepmother treated me (although, at the time, I did not know she was not my biological mother). My dad was an honest man, but he spent most of his time working, and when he was at home, the environment was tense. Our economic situation was very good; in fact, I went to the best schools. However, I always felt that this was not my family.
>
> The only thing that saved me from depression was my relationship with God. When I was just six years old, I would run away from home so I could be at the church. There, I had my conversations with Jesus and received revelations of who He was in my life. The priests told my mother that they thought I

OUR PURPOSE REFLECTS WHO WE ARE,
BUT OUR VISION GUIDES US TO WHERE WE ARE GOING.

was going to be a nun. One of the first revelations I had is that Jesus is alive and not hanging on a cross. After that revelation, I would frequently get angry at the priest and tell him, concerning the statue of Jesus on the cross, "Why don't you get Him down from there? He is not there."

At school, I was a very polite girl with excellent grades. I didn't like going to parties or clubs. I lived between my house, the church, and the school. However, when I was eighteen, something extremely ugly happened to me. I was kidnapped by a man who practiced African witchcraft. He held me captive for almost a year until my parents paid a ransom. This person did sorcery and spells against me. He also abused me, raped me, got me pregnant, and then forced me to have an abortion.

After I was rescued, the effects of my ordeal began to manifest. My parents took me to a priest, prayed for me, and tried to help me become free, but I continued to carry oppression and guilt, and I suffered from eating disorders. I quit my studies, so I didn't graduate. My parents involved me in a business in order to help me, and I turned out to be good at business, so I drowned out all the pain in a new career. In a few years, I became quite successful, traveling the world and earning a lot of money. But the pain inside me was still great. I felt empty, and nothing filled me. I ended up moving away from the Catholic church because I saw many things that were not right. I started looking at other religions, such as Buddhism and Hinduism, but I still couldn't find my way.

When I was about twenty-seven, I went to Latin America on business, and everything went wrong for me. I had a document problem, was scammed in regard to the business I had gone there for, lost all the money I had saved, couldn't leave the country, and became sick. The doctors discovered a serious problem in my uterus and told me that I could not have children. The situation worsened and the problems accumulated. People also did witchcraft against me. I knew that something strong was happening on both a physical and spiritual level, so I made a covenant with God, praying, "Lord, I met You as a child, and I have looked for You everywhere, but I have not found You. If You will bring me back alive to Italy, I promise to obey You."

The next day, when I took a taxi, I found that the driver was a Christian. He told me, "You are a woman of God. Why are you so sad? God has a call for you, but you don't want to obey." I replied, "I don't know what religion you are from, but if you talk to me about Jesus, I will go anywhere." He took me to a church, and the pastor—without knowing anything about my life—told me, "You have a big calling for your land, for Italy, but the devil wants to kill you." They took me to a deliverance retreat, and there I met Jesus again. God set me free, and I had experiences with the Holy Spirit. I was able to forgive my family and even the person who had abducted me. God healed my body, and I began to find solutions to my problems. My business picked up again, and I was able to pay all my debts. Then, God started talking to me about ministering in Italy.

WHEN A PERSON DISCOVERS THEIR PURPOSE, A LEADER IS BORN.

I was so hungry for God that I dedicated myself to seeking spiritual knowledge. I started reading a book by Apostle Guillermo Maldonado and connected with his ministry. After seven years of training in the church the taxi driver had first taken me to, it was time to return to Italy. I went back at the same time that the apostle went to Spain for the first time, and I met him there. God had given the apostle a dream in which he saw my face, and when he spotted me, he recognized me. With the blessing of my former pastors, I placed myself under the spiritual covering of Apostle Maldonado and began my ministry in Rome with a House of Peace of twenty people. There, I met my future husband and got married. God had given me the names of my children, so I never doubted I would become a mother.

That House of Peace multiplied so greatly that today, we have a ministry in almost all the regions of Italy. Ninety percent of the people in our congregation are former Catholics and even former monks. We are also in Germany, Peru, Venezuela, and Spain. We have at least nine hundred leaders under our covering. I am the first Italian woman to be commissioned as an apostle, and this has opened the way for many other women in my nation. God has opened doors for me in politics and on the radio, both locally and nationally, and all this has happened in the five years since the church began. God has used us to restore His people because, in Italy, the percentage of people who are abused is high. Many women have come to the church who have been raped by a family member, and they have psychological, emotional, and physical problems. We have restored them, and now they are women of God.

The Lord has sustained us as a ministry so that I have not needed a secular job. The place where we meet is a miracle; we don't owe any debt on it, and we have everything we need. God has done wonders in our ministry, and we have seen His glory. During the last Supernatural Encounter in Italy, we were able to document 208 testimonies of people who came with cancerous tumors, fibroid tumors, cysts, sciatic nerve pain, and facial paralysis and were completely healed! Many people were also set free from religious oppression.

One of the most notable testimonies was that of a woman who had been a nun. God ministered to her heart so that she could have an encounter with the love of our heavenly Father. She had always wanted to get married, but due to religious norms, she had not been able to do so. Now, she feels like a new person, is full of God's love, and is evangelizing other nuns. I am so grateful to God for everything He has done in our lives. Today, after having gone through so many difficult times, I see His faithfulness whenever I look at the family He has given me, and I am totally in love with Him. I did not know the great purpose God had for my life, but now I can see that everything I went through served to fulfill my destiny in Him.

FROM UNDOCUMENTED IMMIGRANT TO SUCCESSFUL LAWYER

Jesús Reyes arrived in the United States when he was just a child. He grew up in this country, but his status was that of an illegal immigrant. One day, he was detained by immigration officers, but after making a covenant with God, he was freed and found his purpose. Today, he is a well-known lawyer specializing in immigration issues.

> When I was a young boy, there were many political problems in my country, and so my father decided to leave his job and find a better future for his family in the United States. When we moved, I began to have many questions, such as "Why am I here?" and "What will my destiny be in a strange country where I don't know the language or the culture?" Then, I met the Lord. I always wanted to serve Him, but I encountered problem after problem due to my immigration status. Like most undocumented immigrants in the United States, I had many dreams and aspirations, but I didn't have the requirements to stay. Wanting to better myself, I managed to enroll at a university. But one day, I came home to find immigration officers in my apartment. I never thought that would happen to me! Suddenly, I heard someone say, "Come on! You have to leave this country!" I was very afraid. At that time, I was already attending King Jesus Ministry, and I asked God, "Lord, I serve You, and I love You, so why is this happening to me?"
>
> I was taken to one detention center, and then I was transferred to another in Pompano Beach, Florida. After the initial scare, the Holy Spirit filled my heart with faith, and I just wanted to glorify God in this situation. I made a covenant with Him, saying, "Lord, if You take me out of here, I will serve You and Your people." I began to tell my fellow detainees, "Let's glorify

God! Let's dance!" They told me I was crazy. But I answered that God was going to do something.

My mentors and my co-disciples at the church joined in prayer for me. My parents and other family members also prayed for me. I remember that when I was arrested, a lawyer told me what people were doing on my behalf. He said, "Look, they are praying for you. They are doing it with great faith! As they pray, they grab a U.S. residence card and say, "Father, we pray for our brother Jesús Reyes. We pray and decree that he is free, and that You give him the documents he needs to be in this country."

One day, the detainees at my center were out in an open place when, suddenly, we saw a plane come close. It was one of those small planes that can write in the sky with smoke, and the message said, "Trust in God!" For me, that was another sign that the Lord was with me.

Then, inexplicably, I was released from the detention center. How did I get out? I don't know, but it happened. I enrolled at a university and graduated from law school. The Lord paid all the expenses for my studies, amounting to a hundred thousand dollars. When I finished my degree, I worked for a law office until I decided to establish my own immigration law firm. Thank the Lord, I am

AFTER A SUPERNATURAL ENCOUNTER, GOD IS MORE REAL TO US THAN ANY OPPOSITION, PERSECUTION, DISAPPOINTMENT, OR EVEN BLESSING.

now serving His people. Little did I know when I arrived in this country what God's purpose for me would be. He has done supernatural things in my life. Here, I met God, my family was saved, and the dream of a better future was fulfilled—not in my own way, but in God's way.

I have been able to see the glory of God through cases like that of a young Nicaraguan man who came to the United States undocumented, crossing the border through Mexico. He had been fleeing political persecution in his country. U.S. Immigration and Customs Enforcement (ICE) had placed him in a detention center, and he was there for several weeks, with his deportation imminent. He had almost lost hope of being released because the judge had denied him bail. However, by the grace of God, we were able to present compelling evidence that eventually convinced the authorities to release him. He is now a free man in search of the American dream. Also, we had the case of a young man from Guatemala, named Kevin, who had arrived in the United States as a child. He attended school here, growing up under the American educational system. However, one day, the immigration authorities arrested him and took him to a detention center, where he was held for months. His case took more than a year, but finally, with God's help, we were able to free him. Now, he is on his way to obtaining his resident status.

The Lord has led me to become a blessing to others and help them have hope in extreme situations. I thank God for everything I've been through in my life, and I'm waiting for the doors that will open for me next. God does something new every morning in my life, and I can see this in the lives of the people around me. Thank You, heavenly Father, for giving purpose to my life and enabling me to bless the lives of so many people!

ABOUT THE AUTHOR

Apostle Guillermo Maldonado is the senior pastor and founder of King Jesus International Ministry (Ministerio Internacional El Rey Jesus), in Miami, Florida, a multicultural church considered to be one of the fastest growing in the United States. King Jesus Ministry, whose foundation is built upon the Word of God, prayer, and worship, currently has a membership of nearly seventeen thousand. Apostle Maldonado is a spiritual father to 400 churches in 70 countries throughout the United States, Latin America, Europe, Africa, Asia, and New Zealand, which form the Supernatural Global Network, representing seven hundred thousand people. He is also the founder of the University of the Supernatural Ministry (USM). The building of kingdom leaders and the visible manifestations of God's supernatural power distinguish the ministry as the number of its members constantly multiplies.

A national best-selling author, Apostle Maldonado has written over fifty books and manuals, many of which have been translated into other languages. His books with Whitaker House include *Breakthrough Prayer, Breakthrough Fast, Stress-Free Living, How to Walk in the Supernatural Power of God, The Glory of God, The Kingdom of Power, Supernatural Transformation, Supernatural Deliverance,* and *Divine Encounter with the Holy Spirit,* all of which are available in both English and Spanish. In addition, he preaches the message of Jesus Christ and His redemptive power on his international television program, *The Supernatural Now* (*Lo sobrenatural ahora*), which airs on TBN, Daystar, the Church Channel, and fifty other networks, with a potential outreach and impact to more than two billion people around the world.

Apostle Maldonado has a doctorate in Christian counseling from Vision International University and a master's degree in practical theology from Oral Roberts University. He resides in Miami, Florida, with his wife and ministry partner, Ana, and their two sons, Bryan and Ronald.